OBTAINING CITIZEN FEEDBACK:

The Application of Citizen Surveys to Local Governments

by Kenneth Webb
and Harry P. Hatry

The Urban Institute

OBTAINING CITIZEN FEEDBACK:

The Application of Citizen Surveys to Local Governments

by Kenneth Webb
and Harry P. Hatry

The Urban Institute

with contributions from:
Louis H. Blair,
Marvin R. Burt,
Alfred I. Schwartz
and Alease Vaughn

This study was supported by funds from the Charles F. Kettering
Foundation and the U. S. Department of Housing and Urban
Development. The views expressed herein are those of the authors
and do not necessarily represent those of either The Urban
Institute or the supporting organizations.

Library of Congress Catalog Card Number 72-95474

ISBN No. 87766-055-7

UI 121-201-7

Available from:

Publications Office
The Urban Institute
2100 M Street, N. W.
Washington, D. C. 20037

List price: $1.95
Refer to URI-18000 When Ordering

Printed in the United States of America

C/75/3M

Contents

Appendices

EXHIBITS

Acknowledgments

The authors are particularly indebted to Michael S. Lenrow, Director of the Dayton Public Opinion Center, for his cooperation throughout this study. In addition, the Center's Field Supervisor, Thomas Weller, was also a valuable source of information.

Sidney Hollander, Jr., Sidney Hollander Associates; Wayne Anderson, City Manager, Alexandria, Virginia; Harold Goldblatt, Department of Housing and Urban Development; John Parker, District of Columbia Government; Carol H. Weiss, Bureau of Applied Social Research, Columbia University; and Daniel Gottlieb, consultant, contributed many useful suggestions.

In addition, valuable suggestions on various aspects of the study were provided by the following members of The Urban Institute: Donald M. Fisk, Michael Flax, Philip S. Schaenman, Robert Sorrell, Cynthia Thomas, and Joseph S. Wholey.

This report is one of a series prepared by the Institute's State and Local Government Research staff to help officials develop modern and effective management tools. Titles and brief descriptions of other publications in the series are listed in the back of this book.

Summary

Regular surveys of citizens can become an important mechanism by which local governments obtain feedback on public services.

Currently governments are limited in their ability to get a balanced and comprehensive view of citizen thinking on local government issues. Among the common ways that officials obtain feedback are through personal contacts with individuals and groups, complaints, pressures from special interests, editorials and news columns, letters to the editor, and citizen organizations. Useful as these are, they do not easily lend themselves to systematic examination and, generally, they cannot be expected to be representative of the entire population.

Scientifically conducted surveys, however, offer a unique means for officials to test the public pulse—especially on citizen experiences with and perceptions of government services. They are possibly the most, if not the only, efficient way to obtain information on: (1) constituents' satisfaction with the quality of specific services including identification of problem areas, (2) facts such as the numbers and characteristics of users and non-users of various services, (3) the reasons that specific services are disliked or not used, (4) potential demands for new services, and (5) citizen opinions on various community issues, including feelings of alienation toward government and officials.

Such information can be very useful for local governments in setting priorities for resource allocation and the determination of actions to improve existing programs.

Citizen surveys have been used from time to time by many governments to probe many subjects. These have been sporadic efforts and have not begun to tap the full potential of regular

1

surveys. Survey queries based on actual recent experiences of citizens are likely to yield the most dependable and useful kinds of information to local governments.

Regular, annual, citizen surveys that repeat many of the same questions can detect community trends and indicate the magnitude of progress or deterioration in service levels.

This information should be collected and analyzed to show citizen responses from one neighborhood to another and among various population groups of different age, sex, race, and income.

A major obstacle in undertaking widespread surveying in the United States is cost. The cheapest way to survey is by mail-outs to households. Unfortunately, responses to mail questionnaires tend to be highly self-selective and therefore not likely to be representative of the community. Thus, only on survey topics that do not need representative responses, or when it is feasible to compensate for the bias, is the mail survey applicable.

The in-person interview is generally believed to be the most accurate type of survey. It provides opportunity for lengthy, extensive questioning. However, it is also the most expensive.

Gaining considerable popularity among the surveying profession is the telephone survey. It can cut the costs of in-person interviewing. The telephone approach merits consideration where a high proportion of households in the community have telephones. As governments begin to undertake *regular* surveys, it is likely that combinations of these various types of data collection may turn out to be the most efficient way of surveying.

For most issues for which surveying is appropriate, great precision in the findings does not seem necessary. Thus, sample sizes of only a few hundred households (e.g., 500-900), if scientifically drawn, will be representative of the whole jurisdiction. Comparisons of larger subgroups such as major service areas can also be undertaken with such sample sizes.

Costs of about $15 per completed in-person interview (e.g., about $11,250 for a survey of 750 respondents) have been experienced recently for surveys such as described herein. Use of telephone surveys can reduce this by at least $2 per interview. These are probably about as low as possible when an outside organization is used to conduct the survey. Use of internal staff or volunteers can reduce out-of-pocket expenditures considerably, but entail a number of problems. Where such personnel are used, a survey professional should at least guide the survey activity.

Most governments cannot afford to hire full-time survey personnel, even if this were desirable. Who should do the surveying for the government? A professional survey firm can be used; their prices tend to be higher than those indicated above, but the quality is likely to be high. A number of universities have, or are developing, surveys for a wide range of purposes including local government. Their prices also tend to be higher than those indicated above.

Most local governments in the United States cannot afford to wholly support a nonprofit, independent organization (such as the Dayton Public Opinion Center in Ohio, a unique organization established to undertake surveys of *local* issues). This appears to require a minimum of about $100,000 per year. However, as citizen surveys become more widely used by governments and school districts, state or regional support for such organizations is likely to become feasible, assuming cooperative funding commitments from a number of the local governments. This approach would have the virtue of permitting the procurement of a stable professional group of survey designers and interviewers. It could also attain a high degree of credibility, something that is more difficult for a local government that conducts its own surveys on sensitive issues. Regional survey centers should be expected to provide individual service to individual local governments. Fully prepackaged questionnaires are probably not appropriate, though many topics are sufficiently common among governments that some pretested questions are likely to be useful to many local governments. This would permit cross-city comparisons. The federal government and associations of governments might consider how to encourage and support such centers.

Whatever organization is used to actually design and undertake the survey, whether internal or external to the government, rapid response time should be expected. From the time government officials determine and announce the desired topic for coverage until the results become available should be within three months, at least for the type and size survey discussed in this report. Added time will be required for detailed analysis.

Merely tabulating and publishing the responses is not sufficient to make fully productive use of survey information. Governments doing surveying should make provision for in-depth analysis of the responses. Pertinent information obtained from other regular sources of government information such as government records should be considered along with survey information. Only through such analysis can survey information be placed into proper perspective with other types of information to provide accurate and comprehensive guidance to government officials for their decision and policy making.

Unfortunately, there are many dangers in citizen surveys. These dangers, if not alleviated, can not only nullify the value of surveys but actually mislead. Questions to avoid are those which ask the public to express a preference on a subject on which they cannot be expected to be properly informed. Responses may tend to tie the hands of government officials or stampede them into premature action. In addition, poor sampling designs, poorly worded questions, or improper interviewing techniques can lead to intentional or unintentional biases in the responses that can provide misleading responses on any issue. The likelihood of oversurveying citizens and causing large numbers of complaints of being bothered by interviewers is possible, but not likely if the surveying is done by sampling, as seems most practical, and if interviewers are properly trained.

To reduce these important dangers as citizen surveys become more regularly used, provision should be made for periodic audit of the surveying procedures. Such audits should encompass not only the technical aspects of surveys, but also should examine the scope of the questions and the method of release of information to reduce the possibility of important biases.

Despite the authors' enthusiasm for the considerable potential of citizen surveys for providing useful, representative, citizen feedback—available in no other known practical way—that enthusiasm has been tempered by:

1. The numerous dangers and pitfalls that make it quite possible for surveys to be badly misused—to the community, a considerable disadvantage.

2. The lack, at least currently, of perception by local governments of their potential usefulness.

3. The current lack of government analytical capability to utilize fully and satisfactorily the information obtained from citizen surveys.

These problems can be considerably alleviated by:

1.   Use of professional advice and training.

2.   Local government experiments with surveys to test their utility.

3.   The procurement of internal program evaluation and analysis personnel.

The full potential of the use of citizen surveys in a government will not be achieved before these are accomplished.

A shortcoming of current citizen surveys has been the failure to use them extensively to obtain information on specific citizens' *experiences* with particular local public services. Such information can provide major guidance to government managers and officials for policy and program planning and for budget allocations. Instead, the emphasis to date has been on citizen opinions. Though of considerable general interest to officials, such information is often of limited operational use.

Finally, because of the great importance of using citizen feedback in planning and managing, the federal government might encourage local governments to utilize annual citizen surveys as an eligible component of planning or evaluation efforts such as in association with such federally sponsored efforts as Planned Variations, Annual Arrangements, community development and planning block grants. It is such encouragement that will make such vital citizen feedback fully possible.

I.   Introduction

This report explores the potential usefulness of citizen surveys to city and county governments, particularly those undertaken on a regular annual basis. It concludes, with certain cautions, that surveys are likely to become major instruments of local government management in the coming years.

Present Feedback Devices

In all but the smallest and more stable communities where face-to-face contact with the citizenry still survives, the elected officials and chief administrative officers may feel isolated from the community whose needs and wishes they are supposed to perceive. Some sources on which they currently depend for information from citizens between elections are:

- Letters, suggestions, and information from active citizens or special citizen groups.

- The mass communications media.

- Direct communications from individuals or interest groups in the form of complaints, civil suits and petitions.

- Demonstrations or other acts of protest.

- Observation of citizen reaction at various public meetings such as city council sessions.

Despite their usefulness in highlighting individual or group problems, these sources of citizen feedback do not provide a representative picture of how well the government is serving the whole community. Although vocal special interest groups serve a vital purpose, there is a danger that they can be influential at the expense of other groups in the community. The assumption that those who are silent are satisfied is highly speculative and overlooks the possibility that many people feel that their views are not wanted or would not make a difference if expressed, that some simply cannot or do not know how to make their views known, and that still others are reluctant, for personal or political reasons, to speak out.[1]

In an attempt to supplement the existing sources of citizen information, local jurisdictions occasionally have turned to surveys. However, no local government that we have been able to find is currently undertaking regular citizen surveys, and in such a way that trends can be identified. If there are any, they are few in number.

That more has not been done with local surveys is probably due to:

- Lack of perception of the potential usefulness of survey data.

- Lack of familiarity with the current capability of interviewing and sampling techniques.

- Fear that the results of surveys could stir up trouble or build up new demands on officials.

- Concern over costs in the face of tight budget restraints.

National Surveys and Irregular Local Ones

Nevertheless, surveying in general has grown in acceptability and esteem. Much of the popular image of surveying comes from

---

1. A very articulate discussion of the problems of current means for citizen participation is provided in Reference 16, especially pages 741-746.

the work of the political pollsters. The Gallup and Harris polls, for instance, regularly use samples of about 1,600 persons to represent the nation's entire adult population of approximately 130 million people. Yet Gallup has indicated that the results of the last eight presidential elections through 1968 came within three percentage points of the findings in his polls.[2] Industry has long used surveys for market research.

The federal government is increasingly going directly to the citizens for information. The decennial census has been expanded to include a broad range of questions relevant to the provision of services. The federal government also undertakes many regular and special surveys of employment, income, health and, more recently, crime victimization. The data, though primarily available as national aggregates, sometimes are also available by major geographical subdivision.

At the local level, many communities have taken advantage of federal funds to conduct occasional surveys. Several programs of the Department of Housing and Urban Development—Model Cities, "701" General Planning Assistance, and Community Renewal, for instance—have utilized surveys of housing and related issues. Department of Transportation highway planning and research funds are occasionally used for both state and local transportation-related surveys. The Interior Department's Bureau of Outdoor Recreation has provided funds that have been used for surveys concerning leisure facilities and citizen interests. These funds have been used primarily by state governments to assess their park service, rather than by localities.

A study in the fall of 1972 on recreation planning revealed that over 50 percent of the responding local governments (cities over 100,000 and counties over 250,000 population) had con-

---

2. See Reference 6.

ducted surveys of citizens at least once over the past three years on recreation in their locality. The majority indicated that surveys were undertaken at irregular intervals.[3]

Besides these specific use-oriented surveys, broader readings of citizen attitudes have been attempted for the local level. A ten-city survey was sponsored by the National League of Cities' Urban Observatory program in 1970.[4] The same questionnaire was administered in each city (although about half the cities added some of their own questions). It sought to measure citizens' feelings and perceptions about basic local government services and certain features of the city government process itself. Communities also have used various types of surveys as part of "community goals" projects.[5]

The "NEEDS" program of the Health Services and Mental Health Administration of the Department of Health, Education and Welfare has begun to provide technical assistance to 20 to 30 local governments on in-depth surveys of the physical and social environment of their communities as related to health.[6]

Periodic Local Surveys

As to recurring surveys for local governments, much less appears to have been done. UCLA's Los Angeles Metropolitan Area Survey (LAMAS) program has been conducting local area citizen

---

3. See Reference 2.

4. See Reference 17 for a fuller description of the Urban Observatory survey.

5. See, for example, Reference 4.

6. See Reference 20. The citizen survey actually occurs in the second stage of the program with a one-hour interview required.

surveys, covering Los Angeles County twice a year since 1970. Individual local governments can tie into this survey but thus far have not been regular customers.

The Dayton Public Opinion Center (DPOC) which opened in September, 1970, may possibly be the first organization established for the primary purpose of undertaking regular citizen surveys on local issues. It was launched on an experimental basis in Dayton, Ohio to operate for a total of three years with funding support from the Charles F. Kettering Foundation. It has been undertaking regular citizen surveys, several times a year, on a variety of local issues. Thus far, these have been for local governmental bodies and nonprofit public or private groups. The DPOC, with a small permanent staff, uses paid housewives, students, and others as interviewers.

Reasons for This Study

This effort has two derivations. First, a number of Urban Institute projects have been aimed at improving the ability of local governments to measure the effectiveness of their services. In each such project some of the measurements that seemed vital for a proper perspective of service effectiveness required insights into the perceptions of citizens. The citizen survey appears to be the most practical, if not the only, reasonable way to obtain such information.

Secondly, in the spring of 1971 the Kettering Foundation asked The Urban Institute to assess the nationwide potential for the kinds of survey activities being undertaken by the Dayton Public Opinion Center.

This report is based on an examination of the Dayton Public Opinion Center experience in its first one and one-half years of operations, on selected experiences elsewhere, such as the Urban

Observatory ten-city survey, on the published literature on survey sampling (little of this deals explicitly with local government applications), and on Urban Institute experiences with local citizen surveys in other projects. Because of time and money limitations, this does not pretend to be an exhaustive and systematic study of all local government experiences with citizen surveys.

The apparent lack of experience with *regular* (rather than ad hoc) citizen survey efforts by local governments makes the findings necessarily tentative.

This report discusses the various uses of surveys (Chapter 2), their dangers and how to reduce them (Chapter 3), a brief overview and comparison of survey procedures (Chapter 4), survey costs and possible funding sources (Chapter 5), and some organizational options for conducting surveys (Chapter 6). Chapter 7 summarizes the recommendations. Four illustrative examples of survey questionnaires are presented, including one covering a variety of services (Appendix A), and ones offering more in-depth probing in the areas of solid waste collection, recreational services, and local transportation services (Appendices B, C, and D respectively).

As can be noted from the relative lengths of Chapter 2 and Appendices A through D, we believe that the key to citizen surveys for governments is their development for operational use. This will entail a greater orientation of officials to the potency of citizen surveys for improving their local planning and decision making capabilities. It also can serve as a mechanism by which governments indicate their concerns with the viewpoints on, and experiences with, governmental services of their citizens, thus improving the credibility of government in the eyes of the citizens.

Although this research effort focuses on local government, the principal findings appear applicable for the most part to state governments.[7]

---

7. State governments have many direct services to the public. They also often appear to be far removed from the public and may well be in particular need for citizen feedback.

II. Uses of Citizen Surveys

The use of citizen surveys by local government is a relatively recent phenomenon. Their potential has just barely begun to be explored. One cannot, therefore, be comprehensive in listing how they can most fruitfully be employed. Enough surveying has been done, however, to suggest a number of categories of uses and to identify the shortcomings associated with certain types of surveys.

Survey information should be of primary use to public officials in program and policy planning and in resource allocation. Survey findings should help determine budget priorities, identify needed changes in existing activities, and guide the physical location of facilities.

These broad uses are derived from the specific types of information that well designed surveys can yield:[1]

1. Citizen perceptions of the effectiveness of public services, including the identification of problems and gaps in services.

2. Factual data such as the numbers and characteristics of users and nonusers of community services.

3. Reasons for dislikes, or for nonuse, of services.

4. Pretests of citizen demand for new services.

5. Perspectives of community opinion on a wide variety of issues.

---

1. An important additional use for survey information is for *research* purposes—such as to obtain insights into reasons for long-run conditions and to detect citizen behavior and perception patterns. This, however, is likely to be of primary use to research organizations such as universities rather than to local governments.

15

6. Data on citizen awareness of local government programs and the avenues or media by which citizens become informed.

7. A form of citizen participation that can be expected to be representative of citizen viewpoints in the community. (Surveys also might be used to help reduce a sense of isolation or alienation from government.)

The term "public services" as used here encompasses not only the traditional local services such as solid waste collection, police, and street repair, but also the more recent concerns such as housing quality, employment-economic development, equal employment opportunity, and the general quality of life in the community.

At present it seems clear that the survey uses listed above are more potential than actual. Local governments generally do not yet appear to perceive these many uses, or else the rewards of pursuing them are presently outweighed by the anticipated problems of such surveys. Even in Dayton where the Public Opinion Center was partially subsidized and the prices charged were quite low, the usage by local government officials to date has been small.

In addition, desirable analytical skills are generally not currently available within local governments to help in: (a) identifying specific needs for survey information, (b) formulating specific topics for questions, and (c) analyzing the resulting survey data.

The following sections discuss the seven uses listed above in more detail.

Use No. 1   Provide Citizen Perceptions of the Effectiveness of
             Public Services Including the Identification of
             Problem Areas

A promising and relatively untapped use of citizen surveying
is to obtain direct feedback from citizens on the effectiveness of
programs and services. Many quality aspects of government services
cannot be measured in any practical way other than through citizen
surveys. For many local government services, citizen perceptions
constitute a major aspect of service effectiveness.

> ITEM. A recent concern in many local governments is
> citizen perception of police cooperation. One city asked
> respondents—on the basis of actual contact with the
> police—whether police were polite, sympathetic, mean,
> or helpful. The findings could be used as a departure
> point to identify the need for improving police activity
> and the police image.

If surveys are undertaken periodically with at least some
questions repeated each time, the resulting time series can show
whether citizens perceive progress or degradation in the quality of
services, and other trends. Where common questions are used, a
local government could compare itself with national data and with
other local governments.

Since the survey information is intended to feed into program
and policy planning and the budget process, an *annual* flow of information such as is used for workload and cost data seems desirable.
Because of the rarity of regular citizen surveying, this is set forth
as a tentative judgment; less frequent or more frequent surveys may
appear more appropriate after experience is gained.

Special purpose surveys might also be undertaken to help evaluate particular programs. Before a program is initiated, and again after it is launched, citizens may be queried on aspects of the conditions that the program was intended to change.[2]

ITEM. The District of Columbia initiated a special intensive cleanup campaign. A sample of citizens was surveyed both before and after the campaign to determine whether there was a change in their perceptions of street cleanliness. Exhibit 1 illustrates the findings obtained from this effort (see Appendix B for questionnaire used). It indicated that a substantial percentage did perceive some improvement. Of those interviewed, 38 percent felt their streets were somewhat or very much cleaner (Question 2). Actual inspections had indicated that the average street cleanliness had improved only very slightly, though the number of very bad streets had been reduced significantly. Thus there appeared to be a greater perception of improvement in these areas than in the average inspection rating.[3]

If survey data is tabulated by various social or demographic characteristics of the respondents (such as residence location, age, sex, race, and family income), considerably more detailed findings will result. These may give indications to officials of where the need for future attention is greatest.

ITEM. The feeling of security among citizens is an important aspect of the effectiveness of a law enforcement system. In one city it was found that only 21

---

2. See Reference 7.

3. See Chapter 5 of Reference 7 for more discussion of this evaluation.

Exhibit 1. ILLUSTRATION OF PROGRAM EVALUATION FINDINGS

Actual responses to District of Columbia citizen survey (in two service areas of the city) before and after a cleanup program.

QUESTION:		PERCENTAGE RESPONSES	
		April 1971 4 months *Before* Clean Sweep (101 Respondents)	*December 1971* 4 months *After* Clean Sweep (110 Respondents)
(1) What do you think of the cleanliness of the street you live on?			
a.	Clean	14	13
b.	Mostly clean	45	50
c.	Fairly dirty	27	24
d.	Very dirty	14	13
e.	No opinion	0	0
% Satisfied	(a + b)	59 ± 8	63 ± 7
% Dissatisfied	(c + d)	41 ∓ 8	37 ∓ 7
(2) Have you noticed any change in the cleanliness of your streets in the last 3 or 4 months? (Not asked in the April survey.)			
a.	Very much cleaner		10
b.	Somewhat cleaner		28
c.	Somewhat dirtier	not	3
d.	Very much dirtier	applicable	2
e.	No change noticed		52
f.	Don't know/no opinion		5
(3) How often do the collectors spill trash and garbage or leave some that you have set out?			
a.	Hardly ever	64	56
b.	Once a month	8	16
c.	More than once a month	23	26
d.	Don't know/no opinion	5	2
% Satisfied	(a)	67 ± 9	57 ± 8
% Dissatisfied	(b + c)	33 ∓ 9	43 ∓ 8

a. The ranges shown indicate the approximate statistical confidence limits (90 percent).

Source: Blair and Schwartz, *How Clean Is Our City?* Urban Institute, 1972.

percent of a citywide sample felt "safe anytime of
the day to walk around their neighborhood." The
response when categorized by neighborhood showed
a range of from 14 to 28 percent. An objective for the
city's management might be to try to raise the citywide
percentage, perhaps with initial emphasis on those
neighborhoods with the lowest feeling of security. If
regular annual surveying were done, the success of such
actions could be measured. Survey data should be compared with actual reported crime data to provide a better
perspective on the specific actions needed.

Appendix A provides a set of illustrative survey questions, a
large number of which aim at collecting effectiveness data on a
variety of government services. It also illustrates the type of social
or demographic characteristics likely to be useful. Appendices B,
C, and D each illustrate surveys for an individual service—solid waste
collection, recreation, and local transportation, respectively.
Appendix D also illustrates how survey questions can be linked to
specific service effectiveness evaluation criteria.

An illustration of how survey results may be reported is provided in Exhibit 2, dealing with recreation.[4] Analysis of the data
presented would preferably be supplemented by other information
about local recreation. The exhibit itself, however, can be used to
suggest possible interpretations and implications of the data. For
example:

> • Substantial differences in satisfaction among neighbor-
> hoods are expressed. This may mean that the neighbor-
> hoods are not being treated evenly or that their needs

---

4. Exhibit 2 contains survey questions on recreation from Appendices A and
   C. Those questions were recently used by the District of Columbia Recreation Department, but the data used here are hypothetical.

Exhibit 2. ILLUSTRATIVE SUMMARY OF SELECTED ANNUAL RECREATION DATA[1]

| | Neighborhoods | | | | | | | Citywide | |
	I	II	III	IV	V	VI	VII	Current Year	Last Year
Percent of respondents rating neighborhood recreation as poor or fair rather than good or very good. (From Q1)	33	35	35	50	45	60	25	35	45
Percent of respondents who used facilities at least once in the last month. (From Q2)	25	15	30	5	10	6	10	12	10
Percent of respondents who said neighborhood recreation activities were not interesting. (From Q4j)	10	5	15	10	6	20	5	8	20
Percent of respondents who said neighborhood facilities were not open at the right times. (From Q4b)	5	6	7	6	10	15	5	7	10

1. Questions are from Appendix C. Data are hypothetical. A full report should also contain information on the statistical confidence ranges for these numbers.

are quite different. Investigations into the advisibility
of reallocating or seeking added resources for neighborhoods with poorer ratings (e.g., Neighborhood VI)
seem desirable.

- Neighborhood VI also has a relatively high percent of
  respondents who consider the activities not interesting
  and who believe facilities are not open at the right time.
  A thorough review of activities and procedures in that
  neighborhood seems appropriate.

- Improvement appears to have occurred between last
  year and this year. This seems particularly evident in
  the drop from 45 to 35 percent of the respondents
  rating the neighborhood recreation as either fair or
  poor, and in the drop from 20 to 8 percent of those
  who found activities not interesting. This suggests
  that changes made in the past year have been effective according to these criteria.

Use No. 2.   Provide Selected Factual Data

In some instances surveys can be used to provide estimates
of factual rather than perception data. For example, the survey
appears to be a reasonable way to obtain estimates of: (a) the
numbers and percentages of households that use and do not use
such services as recreation facilities and public transit (the resulting information will differ from counts of attendance at a
tennis court or of transit ridership), (b) crime rates—particularly
useful for identifying amounts of unreported crimes and (c)
amounts and length of unemployment and underemployment.

Use No. 3.   Help Identify Reasons for Dislike or Non-Use of Services

Citizen surveys can be used to help officials diagnose why public services or facilities are not liked or not used by certain constituents. Appendix A contains a number of diagnostic questions: why crimes were not reported (Q 12), why public transit was not used (Q 17), why public recreational facilities were not liked (Q 20), why health service was felt unsatisfactory (Q 30), why public health clinics were not used (Q 31). Appendices C and D contain other examples.

When a survey reveals that a significant proportion of citizens are displeased for the same reasons, this pinpoints where corrective action needs to be directed.[5]

> ITEM. A recent citywide survey in the District of Columbia indicated that only 25 percent of the residents used public recreation facilities. The most frequent reason for non-use was a lack of knowledge about the facilities or programs. This suggested a need for more publicity. Note that there may be good reasons for non-use of government facilities (e.g., availability of excellent private facilities). Proper interpretation of survey data will usually require information from other sources.

> ITEM. A Dayton survey was taken to determine usage levels and reasons for non-usage of a recycling center. Of those who had heard of the center but did not use it, only 11 percent thought the location was inconvenient. This

---

5. The questions can also be framed to provide information on the *intensity* of feelings by respondents for each reason.

suggested that increasing the number of recycling centers would not significantly increase usage, and therefore the funds required to establish neighborhood recycling centers probably would produce a higher pay-off if spent other ways. The cross tabulations on this survey also revealed a lower awareness of the recycling center among both blacks and young people, indicating that publicity might be refocused to particular radio stations, programs, and newspapers used by them.

Use No. 4.   Pretests of Citizen Demand for New Services

Market research to test the potential demand for new products has long been a major tool of the private sector. Its use by government, particularly at the state and local level, has been scanty. Well designed surveys, however, could help officials in estimating the demand for and refining the designs of new facilities or services.

> ITEM. Scottsdale, Arizona used a special survey to determine reactions to a new trash collection system involving the replacement of standard trash cans with large multiple-family plastic containers which could be handled mechanically. The survey, built into a pilot test program of variations of the new system, not only provided a measure of citizen satisfaction before and after introduction of the new containers, but also aided in determining that a four-family container was preferred over the two-family model (one reason apparently was that the use of four-family containers disguised the source of the garbage).

> ITEM. A sample of residents could be asked whether they would be willing to pay, say, a dollar more for pick-up of garbage from their yard as opposed to curb service.

To the extent possible, questions asking citizens their preferences towards increased or new public services should provide a clear indication of the anticipated benefits, the likely added cost and impacts—who is going to pay and how—to avoid ambiguous and possibly misleading responses.[6] The two examples above appear appropriate on this basis.

Use No. 5.   Citizen Opinion Surveys

Surveys to gather opinions currently appear to be most popular. Governments seek citizen opinions about:

- Budget or service priorities.

- Existing or proposed ordinances (such as the desirability of Sunday blue laws or dog curbing ordinances).

- Innumerable controversial issues that face government officials.

Examples of questions on service area priorities and on the special issue of citizen "alienation" are illustrated in Section A of Appendix A. The greatest single interest of Dayton city officials in the Dayton Public Opinion Center has been to use the service for obtaining citizen views on city budget priorities.

The United States political system rarely offers the electorate the opportunity for registering an opinion at the ballot box other than in connection with the election of candidates. Conducting a special referendum entails high costs. The more economical sample is thus a tempting device to the local government that wants to sound out public sentiment on various issues.

---

6. Surveys should not be used as a substitute for careful analysis of demand, costs, and benefits involved in altering existing services or providing new ones, but should be used to obtain additional relevant information.

City officials approached during the course of this study expressed most concern about surveys used to gather citizen opinions. Most of them associated citizen surveys as dealing only with opinion polls and they were fearful of the problems described in the next chapter.

Use No. 6.   Provide Data on Citizen Awareness of Local Government Programs

The effectiveness of certain city programs such as recreation, recycling of waste products, and various types of health clinics depends on voluntary citizen participation. It is important for the local government to assess the extent of citizens' knowledge of such programs. Surveys providing this information can help officials gauge the effectiveness of existing publicity efforts and indicate whether corrective action is needed. The *source* of awareness—how citizens learn about public services—can also be determined from survey questions. Information on which media are relied upon, or whether people get information through schools or employers, for example, can be valuable for improving publicity strategies and methods.

Use No. 7.   Provide a Means for Increased Citizen Participation in Government Planning and Policy Formulation, and Reduce Isolation or Alienation From Their Government

The fact that citizen surveys provide one of the few forms of citizen feedback that is reasonably representative of the jurisdiction, indicates that they deserve attention as a form of citizen participation.[7]

---

7. For a relevant discussion of citizen participation, see Reference 16.

In one sense, surveys are a corrective to some other forms of citizen participation that have been criticized for giving undue voice to small minorities, or minorities of minorities. Even if officials happen to be interested only in the views of a particular group, such as the aged, the bus riders, or the residents of a particular neighborhood, a carefully prepared survey may more accurately reflect those views than would some of the means of feedback more commonly relied upon.

It has been surmised that the act of being interviewed might reduce a citizen's feeling of isolation or alienation from his government. However, the basic type of interview that seems most feasible for local governments involves small sample sizes—only a few hundred or a few thousand at most. In a city of 30,000 households (about 100,000 population), an average household would only be approached once every 15 years. So the direct impact of interviewing on those interviewed—even assuming the effects were positive—would have to be considered very small.

Yet, indirectly, citizen surveys might have an impact. If the results of surveys were disseminated often and widely, it would soon become known in a community that local officials were soliciting and discussing the views of all citizens. Presumably, people could read the survey findings and see that people with views like their own (whether in the majority or minority) were counted. How long it would take for this reaction to occur remains unknown. It would seem that the ability of surveys to deal with the complex matter of alienation would not stop short with the process of being asked and being heard. Rather, a crucial consideration is whether officials then appear to act on the findings from surveys. Without prejudging whether that will in fact occur, at least a first step is presenting to public officials certain basic information about people's preferences and experiences that have not previously been available. And perhaps it is not presuming too much to think that the very act of investing in and studying the results of citizen surveys will tend to make officials lean in the direction of dealing with the implications of the findings.

For this study, the authors made a small attempt to measure the effects of citizen surveys on alienation. Survey questions such as Q1, 2, 3, and 4 of Appendix A were added to two of the Dayton Public Opinion Center surveys, approximately six months apart, the first only a few months after the Dayton Public Opinion Center was formed. There was no significant difference in responses on the questions between the time periods. Even if there had been, there would still be the questions as to whether some other factors had caused the change. Clearly, more experience with surveys and in-depth research is necessary before the effects of surveys on alienation can be assessed.

For What Organizational Levels

Survey information as described in the preceding sections should be useful both to "central" and operating agency officials. The feedback from citizens will be an important interest of elected officials, city and county managers, budget and planning directors, and operating agency managers.

An annual survey encompassing a number of government services (to obtain a wide variety of information at minimum cost) seems appropriate for local governments of 50,000 population or over. Appendix A illustrates a multi-service questionnaire to serve a community's general needs.

In addition, the larger departments in local governments may want to survey citizens more in depth on their own area of interest. Annual surveys to detect trends and to make comparisons among segments of the community or with other governments, etc., may be appropriate. Appendices B, C, and D are illustrations of such single function surveys—on solid waste collection, recreation, and local transportation respectively.

In addition, special *ad hoc* surveys may be appropriate for such uses as individual program evaluations, as discussed earlier. Appendix B is an illustration of a questionnaire used for this purpose.

Dissemination of Survey Results

Citizen surveys sponsored by governments are public property. Making the results publicly available—as soon as the government has had an opportunity to examine their contents and is assured that the survey procedures were sound—should establish credibility and may help give citizens a feeling of participation in the process of local government.

The individual responses of particular respondents should be held strictly confidential; only the aggregated data should be released.

Selection of the Specific Subjects for Survey Questions

The method of selection of the specific subjects for survey questions is a major problem, particularly for governments with little previous experience in the analytical use of survey data. Too often, only superficial consideration seems to be given to what data are needed.

Preferably, each government agency that might make use of the survey should carefully identify its overall needs for management and planning information and identify those items for which citizen surveys are a needed source of the information.

Service effectiveness information and certain associated diagnostic questions have already been identified as major candidates for survey topics for inclusion each year. Appendices A through D give a number of specific examples of these. However, individual local governments and their agencies need to review such examples to see if they want and would use the information.

In addition, special issues will arise each year for which citizen feedback can provide important information for public action. Appropriate questions would then be formulated for the annual survey. To identify topics for which survey data would be relevant requires effort on the part of a government.

Survey Data Is Not Enough—Need for Analysis

Tabulations from survey data will be of some immediate use. However, the major payoff to survey data will result if effort is expended to analyze thoroughly the resulting data. Unfortunately, there is a scarcity of analytical staffs in most local governments to help the agencies identify survey topics, and to assist in the analysis of survey findings to make effective use of the data for program and policy planning.

Nevertheless, a start can be made even with existing resources. The following types of analysis are probably desirable at a minimum.

1. Comparisons of responses by households in various parts of the jurisdiction (e.g., service areas) and as classified by various other demographic characteristics—to determine different service levels and needs.

2. Comparisons of responses at different time periods to determine trends and whether progress has been made or whether conditions are worsening.

3.   Comparisons of responses on one question against certain others to help identify possible reasons for various attitudes (e.g., compare attitudes towards facilities against the extent of use of the facilities).

4.   Analysis of information from other sources along with survey data to provide help in policy and program decisions. (Two examples: citizen perceptions of the cleanliness of their neighborhoods could be compared with actual cleanliness inspections; citizen feeling of security should be compared with reported crime rates. In both cases, governments should consider both types of information in determining the type of action required.)

Governments should provide enough effort to analyze the survey data, even if it means cutting back on the amount of survey data collected. As governments apply more analytical resources and gain more experience with analytical approaches, including citizen surveys, their successful and effective use of surveys should increase greatly.

III. Dangers and Pitfalls in Citizen Surveys

Despite their great potential, surveys also present numerous dangers and pitfalls. Government officials should be aware of these dangers and ascertain that they are minimized in surveys they sponsor. Serious errors in judgment and considerable embarrassment to the government can result from surveys if proper caution is not used. Major dangers and pitfalls—and how to avoid them—are discussed in the following sections.

Beware of Opinion Polls on Complex Issues About Which Citizens Lack Information

Opinion surveys have some special pitfalls. Questions have been used, for example, to determine citizen preferences on how tax dollars should be spent and whether certain services should be increased or decreased.

> ITEM. City governments have been tempted to ask respondents such questions as "Which kind of tax do you prefer (or least prefer)?" "How would you rate the job various agencies (each of which is specified) have done trying to control air pollution?" In both of these actual cases respondents clearly did not have nearly enough information on these complex issues to provide meaningful responses. The information provided would need to be used with considerable caution.

> ITEM. When "forestry" obtained the lowest ranking among a selected list of city services, the small budget for tree management was eliminated. Wind storms subsequently blew down trees on streets and there were no forestry crews. Citizens were dissatisfied and the

budget cut resulting from "their" preference was
challenged. The ranks established by the citizen survey,
it then became clear, stemmed from a low citizen under-
standing of vital services in general and of the forestry
function in particular.

The caution about relying too heavily on opinions particularly applies if the choices involve complex issues on which there
has been insufficient public discussion or education. Opinion polls
can be mischievous if misapplied, stampeding government
officials into premature action or tying their hands even if other
information becomes available that suggests a course of action
contrary to survey results. The choice of issues and the wording
of questions thus become extremely important for this class of
surveys.[1]

In only selective instances is it appropriate to ask the local
public directly *what should be done* on an issue. Generally, it
is not fair or responsible to pose this kind of question when
respondents cannot be expected to have sufficient information
to "make" the decision. However, it can be appropriate to test
general citizen feelings on such issues as whether the city should
build a pedestrian mall or establish day care centers. If strong
feelings are expressed, these can serve as valuable guides to
decision makers.

---

1. The New York City Regional Planning Association in the early 1960's
   wanted to use citizens' opinions in developing its regional plan. They
   found that regional issues were too complex for average citizen response
   so they set up workshops of citizens, each with a set of five educational
   meetings. Finally each citizen was surveyed and the information obtained
   was used in constructing the plan. See Reference 40.

   The MIT Operations Research Center took similar steps for its "MIT Citizen
   Feedback Project" for the State Department of Education. Selected citizens
   were first informed about complex educational problems, and subsequently
   surveyed for their judgments and opinions. See Reference 24.

Beware of Citizens' Responses Reflecting Short-Run Considerations to the Neglect of Long-Term Problems

A special problem with citizen opinions is that responses tend to reflect immediate considerations and may be heavily—and excessively— influenced by recent events.

> ITEM. Dayton sampled its citizens in November 1970 and again in October 1971 to rank four alternative emphases for the city budget. Crime had been a major public issue prior to the first survey, but subsequently a large number of employment layoffs occurred in the city. As to be expected, the first survey resulted in clear pressure for a law enforcement emphasis; the second for a job-creation emphasis.

Citizens react to short-term events. The pressure of these events will inevitably affect government officials, too, but it is also clearly their responsibility to have a longer term horizon. They must try to deal with persistent problems that become overshadowed for the general public, and they must try to look ahead to issues that are not yet well publicized.

Beware of Surveys That Appear to Interfere with Elections or Referendums

The temptation may occur to check public opinion prior to a scheduled referendum on an issue. This could be viewed by some interested parties as an attempt to manipulate the results of the ballot box. Surveys generally may have little effect on referendums, but the suspicion that they could is enough to require caution.

Timing of opinion surveys, therefore, is crucial to their objectivity and utility. These considerations argue for the employment of regular annual surveys at a pre-set time of the year, preferably at a time not too near election day, and covering a number of topics.

Beware of Using Surveys to Hide from Controversy and Responsibility

Officials may be tempted to use surveys as an excuse for backing away from controversial issues. To test opinion is legitimate and useful. Yet there are times when the role of a manager or administrator is not to ride with the tide but to exert leadership by trying to change or modify the strongly held opinions of constituents.

Using surveys to justify actions on behalf of a majority while neglecting minority needs and rights is most likely to occur if surveys are applied as quasi-voting devices. This would contradict one of the major intents of citizen surveys—to identify the views not only of the community as a whole but also of particular segments of the population that frequently are ignored or overlooked. This report strongly urges, as a safeguard, that surveys be designed to compare appropriate clientele groups; then any instances of inferior service or unmet need that appear can be highlighted and acted upon.

Beware of Question Wording—What Is Said or Not Said Can Be Misleading

The wording of survey questions is considerably trickier than may appear at first glance. Ambiguities and misunderstandings on wording are a continual danger. Sometimes small, seemingly insignificant, wording changes can affect the responses.

> ITEM. A February 1971 survey asked respondents if they agreed with the statement: "When necessary, fares charged should be supplemented by tax monies to meet

the cost of operating bus services." The June 1971 survey repeated the question but with the words "personal income tax monies" used instead of just "tax monies." In February 50 percent agreed with the statement. In June only 27 percent agreed. This significant shift seems most likely to have been caused by the wording change and not by either a change in citizen attitude between February and June or by the choice of the sample.

Also, survey questions may pose an inadequate choice to respondents. The choice type of question is particularly susceptible to manipulation, either intentional or unintentional.

ITEM: An August 1971 survey asked blacks: "If there were no obstacles, financial or social, would you prefer to live in a black community or in a predominantly white suburb?" It was subsequently recognized that the categories were not complete in the August survey. In the October survey the question included as a further choice "an integrated community." This produced a major shift of responses as shown in the following table:

	August	October
White Suburb	10%	1%
Black Community	68%	30%
Integrated Community	Not Asked	55%
Don't Know	22%	13%

A special wording difficulty often occurs in connection with the use of a checklist of possible reasons for a certain feeling or behavior. If an "other" category is provided, the respondent will have the opportunity to provide a reason that is important but may have been neglected on the list of choices. On the other hand, sole use of an "open-ended" question without any checklist can result in the respondent neglecting, perhaps through forgetfulness, some important category. A combination approach, beginning with an open-ended question that is followed up with a checklist, probably is most desirable if resources permit.

Such pitfalls in question wording can be reduced by using experienced personnel to develop or review questions and then by carrying out adequate pretesting of the questions before the actual survey.

Beware of Sensitive Issues and Questions That Tend to Elicit Silence or Misleading Answers

Citizens are not always able or willing to give their actual reasons for their behavior or perceptions. On sensitive topics, only superficial or erroneous reasons may be given. For issues where this is suspected to be the case, in-depth types of interviews and sophisticated approaches may be necessary. When wording changes or interview techniques cannot overcome this handicap, it is advisable to avoid the question.

Beware of Non-Representative Results If Inadequate Procedures Are Used

A major requirement of a survey is to obtain a representative sampling of households in the community. Considerable care is needed to reduce the possibility of a major bias in the obtained responses. Many distortions in the sample can arise including those from the following causes:

- Exclusion of persons without telephones or without listed telephone numbers in a telephone survey in a jurisdiction where these population subgroups are relatively large and of significance to the objectives of the survey.

- Use of an out-of-date or inadequate listing of household addresses for at-home or mail surveys.

- Reliance on a single member of a household as the respondent to speak for all household members in situations where this is inappropriate.

- Failure to query large segments of the sample because persons refuse to respond or are not at home when the interviewer calls.[2]

In each of these cases, the inability to interview significant segments of the sample might bias the sample. One rough check that can be made is to compare the demographic and socioeconomic characteristics of the persons interviewed against the estimated composition of the total population of the jurisdiction, such as might be obtained from census data or local planning development studies. In addition, design, or at least review, of the survey by a professional is highly desirable to minimize the likelihood of these problems occurring.

---

2. Experience at The Urban Institute has indicated that advanced mailing of a letter of introduction seems to improve the response rate, at least for telephone interviews.

Beware of Antagonizing Citizens Who Consider Interviews an Invasion of Privacy

Some citizens may object to being interviewed. Proper interviewer behavior towards persons being asked to respond should alleviate much of this. In fact, many people like to be interviewed as it gives them a chance to talk to an intent listener.

Some questions may provoke resistance, but there is little evidence of generalized objections to surveys. Even on personal questions such as income, the great majority of those interviewed provide a response. (Based on the Dayton Public Opinion Center and Urban Institute experiences, about 85 percent or higher respond to the question on income particularly if the respondent is asked to select one of a small number of income groupings rather than to give a specific figure.)

In some instances, persons may be afraid to respond, particularly for in-person interviews. A recommended practice is to notify the police department about a survey before interviewing begins. Then citizens wishing to check the legitimacy of the survey can do so by calling the police.

Another type of problem—annoyance— will arise if a person feels he is being interviewed too often. However, as noted in Chapter 2, with the small sample sizes considered most appropriate for local governments, any given household is not likely to be interviewed by the government more than once every several years.[3]

---

3. Reference 7 reports that 35 percent of 1,004 respondents interviewed in July 1966 had been interviewed at least once before in their lifetimes. This was based on a national probability sample. Eighteen percent of those previously interviewed considered parts (mostly income questions) of the interviews to be an invasion of privacy. We do not know the form in which the question on income was asked.

Responses to surveys by citizens must be voluntary if they are to have validity. Care should be exercised not to mislead persons into thinking that they are required to respond.[4] Also, individual responses need to be safeguarded. Perhaps special local ordinances may be needed to protect against improper release of information on individual responses.

Beware That Dissemination of Survey Findings May Be a Two-Edged Sword, Raising False Hopes Among Citizens and Providing Political Fodder to Candidates

The dissemination of findings may serve to raise the level of citizen expectations. The findings themselves also may be used as political ammunition. To some these results are good, to others, bad. It depends a good deal on whether one is seeking change and reforms or defending the status quo, whether one views controversy and public discussion as challenging opportunities or as bothersome circumstances to be avoided, whether one prefers constituents to be apathetic or involved, and whether or not one tends to have faith in an informed public.

In any case, government officials should expect that citizens may become more demanding in seeing improvements made as surveys highlight the need or desire for them. Pressures to manipulate the data rather than to improve conditions may occur. Certainly, candidates for election—among the "ins" as well as the "outs"—will attempt to use citizen survey findings to their own advantage.

To make proper use of citizen surveys, officials need to assure that defensible survey procedures are used since these are likely to come under attack by those who do not like the findings. As already noted, regular surveys should not be conducted at periods close

---

4. The point was emphasized in Reference 34 (Chapter 7 on "Findings and Recommendations on Privacy and Confidentiality").

to election time. Survey designers should avoid questions that unreasonably tie the hands of government officials or stampede them into questionable actions. We also stress that the complete results should be made available to the public. Releasing only partial results, or perhaps only the government's interpretation of them, may lead to suspicion and reduced credibility, not only in one survey but in surveys generally.

Survey Audits—A Means of Reducing Dangers and Increasing Credibility

One of the best defenses against many of the risks cited is to provide for periodic audit of a local government's survey procedures. The audits could be conducted by professional organizations that have expertise in survey procedures and by nonpartisan or bipartisan civilian panels. They should look especially for biases that might have slipped into the community survey through sampling techniques, subject choices, interviewing techniques, or data tabulation, and into the methods of release information. Even before some sensitive surveys are launched, approval of questionnaires or participation in their formulation by citizen advisory panels may be worthwhile safeguards.

Any finding of significant bias, attempt to manipulate public opinion, or other abuse of impartial survey purposes identified during the audits would need to be corrected promptly. The audits will be beneficial in two principal ways. First, they will permit the government to have greater confidence in the meaningfulness of the survey findings. Second, they will create greater credibility for the survey work in the community at large.

IV. Survey Procedures

This study was not intended to explore in detail the various methods of undertaking surveys.[1] However, a brief review of some of the major elements of surveying is intended to give local officials a better perspective of the nature of surveys.

Exhibit 3 presents the typical major steps in the survey process. Deciding on topics for the survey (Step 1), analysis of findings (Step 9), and the uses of the information (Step 10) are each briefly discussed in Chapter 2.[2] Costs are discussed in Chapter 5. This chapter primarily discusses the various surveying modes (Step 2) and the pretesting and training of interviewers (Step 6). The chapter ends with a brief discussion of the calendar time required for surveys.

Modes of Survey

The three traditional ways of conducting citizen surveys are the personal face-to-face interview, the telephone interview, and the mailed, self-administered form. The personal face-to-face interview is generally believed to produce the best return but is generally the most expensive. The telephone survey is somewhat less expensive, but the problem of households without telephones can lead to a sampling bias. The mail technique is least expensive, but produces a smaller percentage of responses and therefore its credibility as an unbiased procedure is low. Combinations of modes may be appropriate but can complicate the procedures.

---

1. References 18 and 21 discuss many of the important elements of surveys of most concern to local governments. For more in-depth technical discussion, relevant material will be found in References 22 through 31.

2. There is little in the published literature on these topics for use by local governments.

44

Exhibit 3. TYPICAL STEPS IN THE SURVEY PROCESS

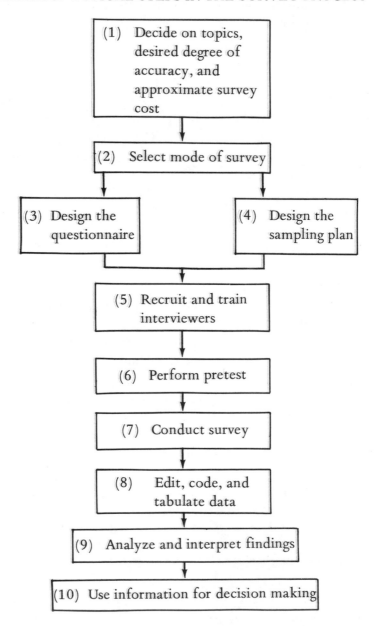

Mailed, Self-Administered Survey

Marked differences of opinion appear in the literature on the representativeness of the population of mailed surveys. A number of studies indicate that the mailed questionnaire is not a valid survey method for any but highly selective situations.[3] These studies report significant differences between those who do and do not respond to mailed questionnaires. Thus the answers received cannot be assumed to reflect the responses not received. A method to reduce possible bias from non-respondents has been to follow up with more mailings, telegrams, phone calls, and house visits. Mail surveys also require a fair degree of literacy on the part of respondents.

Advantages of the self-administered questionnaire are:

- It can have more candid results because it is done in privacy (and can be anonymous).

- It is done in the comfort of the home and is not subject to the stress of the interview.

- It is generally inexpensive.

Self-administered mail surveys are most likely to be appropriate where the population sample is highly motivated to respond or where a strong case can be made that those who respond are the primary group from whom the information is wanted.

A means of carrying out mail surveys in some jurisdictions is to attach the questionnaire to a utility bill. The cost is minimal, mainly the cost of printing and analyzing the information

---

3. See, for example, References 33 and 35.

46

when the questionnaire is returned. Response rates, however, can be very low, sometimes going below 10 percent.

> ITEM. A 1970 Charlotte, North Carolina recreation survey was included in 70,000 water bills. There were 5,087 replies (7 percent) that could be used.

> ITEM. Winnetka, Illinois obtained a 25 percent response on an attachment to utility bills.[4]

Another variation of the self-administered survey is to insert the questionnaire form in the local newspapers.

> ITEM. College Park, Maryland obtained a 15 percent household response on a survey of alternative financing proposals and ranking of quality of city services by inserting a survey form in the local newspaper.[5]

Telephone Interview Survey

The telephone interview appears to be an increasingly used method of survey because of relatively lower cost, ease of administering, and ability to reach most of the population.

This method of survey can be subject to bias for citizens who do not have telephones. In Washington, D.C., for instance, 9 percent of the households do not have telephones. This percent can vary, however, among various segments of the population. In Dayton, samples indicate a 14 percent phoneless rate for households in the Model Cities area compared to a 5 percent phoneless rate in affluent areas. The possible effects of bias from unreachable households should be examined carefully when the survey is

---

4. See Reference 43.
5. See Reference 25.

planned. After the survey is completed, the survey demographic data can be compared with census data or local planning data if available to determine if segments of the population are under-represented. Weights can be used to adjust if appropriate.

There is an increasing trend to unlisted numbers. In fact, *Parade Magazine* of March 26, 1972, published the following estimates of phone users with unlisted numbers: Washington, D.C., 25 percent (of total phones); Los Angeles, 33 percent; San Francisco, 23 percent; and New York City, 21 percent.

Thus, sampling from the telephone book can miss a con-siderable portion of the households (and will oversample multiple-phone households). In Washington, D.C. telephone sampling data indicate that less than 68 percent of households would be included in the list from which the sample is drawn if the telephone book is used.

A currently popular way to reduce the problem of unlisted numbers is to use "random dialing." Random four digit num-bers are assigned to each telephone exchange in the locality. Each is dialed for interviews. Many nonresidential and non-working numbers will be included and need to be screened out.

Telephone surveys can utilize nearly all types of questions with the advantage that the respondent is at ease in his own home. Questions where visual displays are required are, of course, not possible. The length of interviews that are possible appears to be surprisingly long. In our own telephone survey efforts we have been trying to keep the average time under fifteen minutes, but much longer interviews have been success-fully completed.

The success of the telephone interviewer is dependent largely on the voice that is projected, so the choice of individual is very important. Female interviewers have shown greater success in limited tests at the Institute. Personable, enthusiastic people have been the most successful interviewers.

The sources of phone interviewers may be volunteers, employees, and temporary hires. Volunteers may be difficult to recruit and control. Use of city employees may interfere with operations. The paid temporaries are the easiest to use. There is a side benefit in using regular employees, however, in that they may learn from talking to the public, increasing their awareness of problems. They also give the public the feeling of being paid attention to by their government. The Urban Institute has participated in successful telephone surveys on recreation using municipal recreation department employees. They blended their normal normal work loads with the interviews that they conducted both on work time and in the evenings.

A telephone survey requires fairly extensive training sessions to guarantee the proper pace and quality of interview. This has been accomplished in four-hour training sessions where proper techniques are taught and the trainees perform trial interviews under the direction of the teacher. Training is especially important if the interviewers are not to be monitored during their interviews, but do their interviews at their own office or at home. (Quality control checks are nevertheless still desirable—by calling back a sample of respondents.) It is, however, preferable to undertake telephone surveys from a central office where interviewing can be monitored by a supervisor.

Personal Face-to-Face Interview

The face-to-face personal interview is probably the most informative of the survey methods because visual aids can be used.

The flexibility in personal interviews is a main asset especially for research type problems. The interviewer can present visual material and make observations of the respondent and his house where appropriate. The high rate of response usually associated with house-to-house interviewing has not been obtained in some inner city surveys where the people are afraid to open their doors.[6]

It has generally been felt that personal interview yielded the best samples because it can reach everyone in the population. However, most of the personal interview sampling has depended on lists of households or lots. Recent telephone survey and personal interview comparisons show that more of the young and very old are reached by telephone, whereas the personal interview method under-sampled these categories.[7]

The costs and manning for face-to-face interviews are usually higher than other methods.

Overall Comparisons of the Three Survey Methods

Comparisons of the three methods of interview can be summarized graphically as follows:

Interview Method	Predicted Results	Cost
Face-to-Face Personal	high response	high
Telephone	some sampling inadequacies	medium
Self-Administered Form	lowest percent returns, possible major biases	least expensive

---

6. See Reference 41.

7. Source: Unpublished computer runs of the Dayton Public Opinion Center.

These generalities, however, have to be considered in the light of each particular survey problem. The selection of the survey mode is usually based on the analyst's estimates of the seriousness of the possible bias effects, the costs, and the available funds.

Pretest and Training

It is too much of a risk to ignore pretest of the questionnaire and training of the interviewers when organizing a personal interview or telephone survey. Pretesting is essential to selecting the form of question that produces the most dependable results. Vague answers, confused responses, high returns of "don't know," and other poor results are symptoms that can be corrected prior to the full survey. There are usually several phases:

Phase I. Experimental choice of questions for the questionnaire can be tried out in a few interviews by an experienced interviewer.

Phase II. A "pretest" form is prepared, that is, one that is ready for formal testing. This is tested on a small sample of citizens to correct poor questions.

Phase III. Training of prospective interviewers can take place with a pretest form or the final version. Training encompasses at least four hours of practice interview and instruction by a professional. Interviews by each person are studied to look for high rejection rates, poor completions, and other poor performance. Interviewers are selected for the actual survey on the basis of producing the least of the negative factors.

To some extent the survey form and the interviewers can affect each other. For instance, if the interviewers are inexperienced, the survey forms may require many instructions and perhaps less intricate question methodology.

Time Required for a Survey

The time span required, once it is determined to do a survey and until the final report showing tabulations is written, is often critical to government officials. Surveys that do not provide results for many months, as may happen, will often be less useful: the results may be too late to have a bearing on decisions, and the findings, if quite old, may no longer hold true. The Public Opinion Center in Dayton generally has processed surveys in about two to three months, measured from the time the survey was first requested until a report with tallies on each question was provided. This time applies to both in-person and telephone surveys. Note, however, that extensive reviews of survey topics and questions were not held, although pretesting was undertaken. The total time will depend heavily on the clarity of issues defined by the government officials, the number of reviews required, and the urgency expressed. A local government using relatively untrained in-home personnel to any significant extent should probably allow closer to three calendar months. When the same questions are repeated in consecutive surveys and the interviewing personnel are experienced, the time can be shortened.

Full analysis of the data, however, is likely to extend well beyond three months to exploit all of the tabular data for decision making purposes. The analysis and integration of the data by management into the decision making process depends on the type of issue surveyed, the complexity of the actions or policies being contemplated, and the priorities attached to the effort— all of which can vary so much that a time estimate would serve little purpose.

Exhibit 4. COSTS FOR FOUR IN-PERSON SURVEYS AT
THE DAYTON PUBLIC OPINION CENTER

	Surveys			
	1 Sept. 1971	2 Oct. 1971	3 Nov. 1971	4 Feb. 1972
Data Collection				
Pretest	$ $ 36	$ 48	$ 53	$ 46
Interviews and Travel	2,720	2,981	2,254	1,936
Office help	140	488	310	195
Training costs	156	126	66	65
Field supervision	636	685	439	274
Printing	97	309	204	198
Data Processing and Tabulation				
Coding	552	1,028	441	416
Computer & Keypunching	499	611	514	641
Total Variable Cost	$4,836	$6,276	$4,281	$3,771
Total interviews completed	696	803	697	805
Average interview time (minutes)	35	35	25	15
Variable costs per completed interview	$ 6.95	$ 7.82	$ 6.14	$ 4.69
Prorata share of fixed costs[1]	$ 6.70	$ 6.70	$ 6.70	$ 6.70
Total Cost Per Interview (excluding start-up costs)	$13.65	$14.50	$12.80	$11.40

1. Based on the assumption that the fixed costs of about $40,000 per year should be spread over 8 surveys per year at an average of 750 interviews—or 6,000 total interviews per year. If fewer surveys are undertaken, this unit cost would rise.

V. Costs and Funding Sources

The cost of surveys is necessarily a major concern for most local governments. The factors determining cost include the method of interview, the sample size, the length of interview, the type of questions, and other operational aspects of the survey. But some of these same factors, particularly the interview method and size of sample, also affect the accuracy and precision of the survey statistics. Reference 16 discusses a number of the relevant aspects of the relationship among costs, accuracy and precision, and survey characteristics.[1] We will not repeat these here, but rather will focus on updating the cost information based on such experiences as those of the Dayton Public Opinion Center (DPOC).

Cost Categories

The costs detailed here refer at first to personal face-to-face interviewing. The adjustments for phone surveys are discussed later.

Start-Up Costs

If existing facilities and equipment can be used, start-up costs will be minimal. DPOC made use of rented quarters but required funds for remodeling and for furniture. Certain other start-up costs, such as initial training or moving expenses of the staff, will depend on the prior training, experience, and source of the staff. DPOC required about $9,000 for these start-up items.

Fixed Annual Costs

The fixed cadre and other non-variable elements will vary according to the size of the operation. DPOC fixed costs include

---

1. The trade off between precision and sample size is illustrated in Appendix **F**.

the salary of the director, salaries for part of the time of the field and office supervisors, and office costs such as rent (to house two full-time and eight part-time staff). These cost about $40,000 annually. Salary levels, of course, can vary considerably, depending on the location and the amount of experience and reputation sought.

Variable Costs

The costs of planning, sampling, developing questionnaires, printing, training, interviewing (both pretest and operational interviews), data processing, and analysis vary considerably with sample size and mode of interview. As Exhibit 4 indicates, DPOC costs on four recent in-person surveys show a range of from about $5 to $8 of variable cost per completed interview.[2] These were for sample sizes of 700-800 households and interviews of 15-35 minutes. These are roughly the sample sizes foreseen for the surveys discussed in this report.

Total Cost

As Exhibit 4 indicates, the total cost per interview in Dayton including a prorata share of fixed costs was about $11 to $15. For a sample size of 750, on this basis, an in-person survey would cost from about $8,000 to $12,000.

---

2. DPOC uses a special type of household selection in which callbacks (at homes where interviews were sought but did not take place) are avoided. However, there is a quota on the number of each sex and age category to be interviewed. This procedure derived from the Gallup organization. An illustration of the resulting statistics are the figures for the DPOC February 1972 survey. There were 2,590 visits to different homes. Of that number, 805 interviews and 272 refusals resulted. This leaves 1,785 homes where no one answered the door or the required respondent was not home. Interviewing costs are quite sensitive to the number of callbacks undertaken, so survey procedures that necessitate callbacks may increase survey expenditures considerably.

The effect of using telephone interviews would be to reduce the interview, travel, and field time by roughly one-half. Other costs would remain about the same. This would result in a pre-interview cost of about $2 less per interview (about $9 to $13 each) and a total cost for 750 telephone interviews of about $7,000 to $10,000.

Some comparison figures are provided in References 16 and 20. The former shows a "low" cost of about $11 to $12 per in-person interview for sample sizes of between 500 and 1,000 interviews. Its "moderate" cost estimate was about $20 to $22. The "high" estimate was $32 to $40 per interview, this being the possible cost for a very sophisticated sample design and process. The DPOC's recent experience places it near the low end of the estimates. The same reference gives approximately $17 per interview as the "moderate" estimate for telephone surveys of 500 interviews.

The DPOC costs, we suspect, are about the lowest possible for quality surveys. Many survey organizations are likely to charge at least twice as much.

The costs indicated in this chapter do not include the cost of the time of government personnel in initially formulating the topics to be covered by the survey. Nor do they include the cost of time that should be applied by local government personnel to analyze survey findings after they became available.

The following table shows the man-hours required for interviewing and field supervision for four recent Public Opinion Center surveys:

Activity	Survey Number			
	1	2	3	4
Interviews	1,039	980	700	612
Crew Chiefs and Field Supervisor	244	267	169	122
Total Man-Hours	1,283	1,247	869	734
Sample Size	697	803	697	805

Source: Dayton Public Opinion Center records.

In addition, approximately 500 man-hours were required for each survey to code the answers preparatory to keypunch.

Reduced Cost Approaches

Actual out-of-pocket costs can be reduced by using in-house personnel or volunteers for many of the surveying activities. These options present some problems (see Chapter 6). Where in-house or volunteer personnel can be used for interviewing, data processing, and other tasks, use of a professional consultant to guide the surveying activity is strongly advised. This could reduce the actual out-of-pocket cost to the government to $1,000 to $5,000 for an entire survey.

Some very low cost surveying approaches also are possible. Most take the form of mailed self-administered surveys. As Chapter 4 has discussed, most are highly suspect with a variety of forms of bias. It will be recalled that with a small questionnaire attached to a utility bill, the cost is minimal (mainly for printing and analyzing the information) but response rates are very low.

Possible Funding Sources

In addition to local funding sources, support for citizen surveys may come from a variety of federal planning-related programs. Local officials can seek financing for surveys from such programs as HUD's Planned Variations, and "701" planning assistance, and from the Department of Transportation and Bureau of Outdoor Recreation planning funds, as appropriate for survey topics and purposes. In addition, the Department of Health, Education and Welfare, the Office of Economic Opportunity, and the Department of Labor are encouraging evaluation efforts for their own programs. Citizen survey feedback as discussed in Chapter 2 could become a major source of such evaluation information and might qualify for funding on that account. The Department of Health, Education, and Welfare "NEEDS" program, though not providing funds, can provide some limited technical assistance.

The Dayton Public Opinion Center has attempted to develop paying customers from the local governments in its vicinity. Thus far in its first 21 months of existence it has not been very successful. Only the Dayton city government has been a significant source of funds. The city provided a total of about $16,000 for their participation in three surveys. Of this, $12,000 was supported by the federal Planned Variations program.[3]

In addition, local government survey funding could be supplemented from sources such as news media, civic agencies, and businesses in the community. Care must be taken, whatever the funding source, to assure that the public interest and independence of the survey operation are not compromised.

---

3. The next largest amount received by DPOC was $3,000 from a local newspaper for providing a weekly column over a six-month time period. Each column described the survey results of one or two questions that were felt to be of particular interest to the newspaper readers. The Center did not feel it was staffed adequately to renew the contract.

VI. Organizational Options for Undertaking Surveys

There is no substitute for trained technicians in survey work. Local governments should attempt to use trained people whenever possible for advice or to work on the survey project. Yet only the very largest local governments are likely to be able to support their own full-time in-house survey research group. State governments probably could afford their own, but should consider using the state university system, some of which already have major survey capability.[1]

The options discussed below pertain to those local governments where complete in-house staffing either is not feasible, desirable, or necessary. Some of the options can be used in combination.

Outside Consultants and University Specialists

Private organizations and universities often can provide the technical expertise to undertake or guide survey procedures according to responsible and acceptable standards. Employing these professionals probably requires the least effort by the local government. The main problem is the high cost. In addition, if localities do not have a firm or university with survey capability in their immediate vicinity, they must go farther afield for assistance. Then, unless the same professionals are used regularly, time will be lost while they seek to familiarize themselves with the relevant local conditions. As noted above, state governments might use the state university system capability (also at a cost), though in many cases survey capability may not currently exist and would have to be developed.

---

1. In New Jersey for instance, there is a statewide New Jersey Poll at Rutgers University. Under contracts to state agencies and statewide TV and radio, surveys are performed on a variety of state issues.

Government Employees

Local governments that are under tight budget restraints will find the option of using existing public employees for survey work particularly attractive for economy reasons, assuming only intermittent effort is required so the normal work functions do not suffer.

Government employees generally can assist most readily and satisfactorily with data processing and interviewing. Design of the surveying procedures should still be handled by experts. Yet internal analytical staff may become proficient enough as they gain experience in survey design to reduce the amount of outside consulting required.

There are certain disadvantages of using government employees. They probably need to be trained each time a survey is made, unlike those in an organization with a stable group of interviewers. Other duties may take public employees away from their interviewing or these other duties may be disrupted by the possibility that public servants may feel personally involved or threatened by the survey questions. This may affect the responses of the citizens they interview.

For these reasons, special attention to quality control of the interviewing is necessary under this option. The interview activity should be explicitly assigned as a regular work assignment. Some compensatory time may be needed for interviewing done outside regular duty hours. Interviewing on off-duty hours is likely to be necessary to locate respondents at home.

ITEM. District of Columbia recreation department employees recently were used to make telephone interviews about city recreational services. Although this arrangement worked reasonably well, all of the difficulties noted above did appear at one time or another.

A special example of relying on public employees is the use of school teachers to help with surveys of parents. This is a relatively undemanding type of assistance when the teachers' responsibility is simply to give out questionnaires to pupils to take home to their parents and return when completed.

> ITEM. An early 1972 parent survey by the Arlington County, Virginia School Board used this procedure. All 15,000 households with children in the public schools were included in the sample. A 67 percent return rate was obtained. The forms were placed in an envelope with a cover letter explaining the purpose of the survey. Appendix E is a copy of the cover letter.

A final problem is that the credibility of a completely government-run survey may come into question.

Volunteers

Use of volunteers has most of the same advantages and disadvantages as using regular government employees. The cost is even less expensive because they are not taken away from their regular duties. However, volunteers are not subject to the discipline of employees and therefore dependability is likely to be a particular problem. Screening and training is needed each time a survey is undertaken. A higher percentage of "dropouts" and non-completions can be expected, requiring others to take on the load. We do not recommend this for regular surveying, but in some instances the cost savings may make this the only practical option.

ITEM. The League of Women Voters in Arlington
County, Virginia provided the interviewers for a 1972
survey of citizen experiences and attitudes towards
various aspects of the county's criminal justice system.
Initially, 24 volunteered; 15 completed their quota
of interviews. Most of the interviewers had no prior
interviewing experience. A paid consultant was used
to design the survey, train interviewers, and oversee
the interviewing. Good results were obtained; for
example, the refusal rate was only 9 percent.

Completely Independent Survey Organization

Another option is to have surveys initiated, conducted, and
financed completely independently of the local government, as
by a municipal research bureau. The principal advantage would
be that the credibility of the survey work would tend to be higher
than if a local government itself controlled surveys about its own
operations. The principal disadvantage is the possibility that an
independent survey operation might not adequately reflect the
needs of the government in either question coverage or timing.
In addition, funding would be difficult to obtain. (If the local
government provides support and initiates survey topics, these
problems would be alleviated—but in that case the option becomes
essentially the same as that discussed above under "Outside Consultants and University Specialists.")

If the thrust of the survey is to obtain information on citizens'
past experiences with particular government services (for effectiveness measurement and as clues to improvements that are
needed—as discussed in Chapter 2), as contrasted with the public
opinion type question (particularly on sensitive issues), then the
credibility issue may well *not* be a major one. The information
obtained in the first type of question is basically management-

oriented data that government officials can use along with other more traditional publicly collected information.

Hired Nonprofessionals

Housewives, college students, and even high school students may be a source of relatively inexpensive help on surveys, especially for interviewing.

> ITEM. Tucson used college students in 1965 for five surveys of 600 citizens each for a cost of only $700 for each survey.[2]

A Possibility for the Future: Regional Citizen Survey Service Centers

As citizen surveys are used more frequently by a larger number of governments, another option will become feasible: regional survey organizations are likely to become viable. Such organizations could service school districts and various regional planning bodies as well as city and county governments in the region.

The Dayton Public Opinion Center offers the first example, of which we are aware, of a nonprofit survey operation designed primarily to serve local governments.[3] It has done surveys for the county, the cities within the county, and the school district. However, these have not been sufficient to support its existence without foundation funding support. Its scope thus far has been limited for the most part to the county area. Regular uses by

---

2. See Reference 5.

3. However, there are many nonprofit research organizations that occasionally do survey work for local governments or are willing to.

the local governments have not yet developed, and government funding pinches have exercised added constraints.

Based on DPOC experience, an estimated $100,000 per year is the minimum amount required for such an operation. This would permit a stable core professional group for survey design and interviewing. Such survey centers should be expected to provide "personalized" service to individual governments. Surveys should be tailored to individual need. Yet individual governments should enjoy some cost savings when they make use of questions already tested in other jurisdictions. The use of equivalent questions would permit cross-city comparisons.[4]

In addition to the nonprofit organization established solely to undertake local surveys (such as Dayton Public Opinion Center), another mechanism to consider is the university-based survey center. Some of those currently in existence already have a regional base. Their responsiveness to local governments (particularly since their customers are not limited to local government) and costs, would be major concerns to work out. Such an organization would probably also have a high degree of credibility, particularly if its own procedures were periodically audited as has been suggested elsewhere.

---

4. The repeating of questions in annual surveys will also reduce other costs (such as pretesting). For telephone interviews, the use of special telephone service such as WATS lines offers an additional type of economy to regional centers.

VII. Conclusions and Recommendations

The citizen survey in the future can become an important government management tool for providing citizen feedback to local officials. Surveys have substantial limitations, however. Data and findings from them should contribute to, but not substitute for, political and managerial judgement. The data need to be analyzed along with other information rather than being considered self-sufficient for planning, policy, and program decisions.

Surveys have dangers that need to be recognized and minimized. Opinion surveys based on inadequate information can give misleading signals. Surveys held too close to elections can become political footballs. Surveys with poorly worded questions may give citizens false expectations of government action and the published results may tie the hands of local officials.

Surveys can provide a degree of citizen participation by fairly reflecting and disseminating the views of all the people. Letting people be heard—minorities as well as majorities—is only one aspect of citizen participation. Its ultimate success in helping to reduce a sense of alienation from government depends on the degree to which survey findings are translated into action by local officials.

While the use of surveys generally is growing, pointing to an almost inevitable increase in their application to local government problems, this tendency will be held back until public officials have a greater awareness of the potential assistance they can derive from citizen surveys.

A further limitation on the use of surveys by local governments is the lack of training among local public employees in the design, procedures, and analysis of surveys.

Citizen surveys are not an end in themselves. They should not be undertaken unless public officials and managers are willing and able to finance them adequately, formulate them carefully, and analyze their findings thoroughly.

A rough rule of thumb is that surveys should cover several hundred households and allow for about $15 per interview. These estimates must be modified according to the nature of particular surveys. Out-of-pocket costs could be reduced considerably by using existing personnel for some survey tasks.

Many conclusions and recommendations about citizen surveys probably apply to state as well as to local governments.

Recommendations for Individual Local Governments

1. Local governments should consider undertaking regular annual citizen surveys. Emphasis should probably be on data on citizens' perceptions and experiences with individual public services. Questions to identify reasons for dislike and for non-use should be included to help identify service deficiencies. Certain questions should be repeated to detect trends. Illustrative surveys such as those contained in Appendices A through D could be used as a starting point for a government's own surveys.

2. Survey information should be collected and tabulated according to geographic and socioeconomic categories to permit officials to check service quality and needs for various population segments such as different neighborhoods, age groups, income classes, and other categories of the population.

3. Individual government departments (at least the major ones that provide direct services to the public) should be major participants in the identification of citizen survey topics that would

provide information relevant to policy or program planning. They should also participate in the review and interpretation of the information obtained from the survey. Individual departments should consider their own separate surveys only if their data requirements cannot be incorporated into the larger survey design.

4.   High level local officials such as the mayor, city or county manager should explicitly examine the scope of a proposed survey to assure that it covers major interests of the government in a reasonably objective manner. They should subsequently obtain detailed briefings on survey results, especially to identify desirable follow-up action indicated by the results.

5.   Local governments that carry out surveys have two important dissemination tasks. They should make certain that survey information is delivered quickly to interested and responsible persons within the government, along with related information that will aid in interpretation. And, in general, they should make the data fully available to the public. At no time, however, should the confidentiality of individual responses be violated.

6.   Local governments should develop in-house capability for utilizing surveys, assigning at least one person to coordinate the effort. However, outside consultants will usually be needed at least to design the survey and train interviewers. Regular government employees might be utilized, especially for nontechnical tasks, to reduce cash outlays.

7.   Local governments should seek audits of their survey efforts by outside professionals and by citizen panels to guard against misuse and to enhance credibility.

Recommendations for Associations, Foundations, and the Federal and State Governments

1.   Associations of government, federal and state governments, foundations and universities should conduct research in local government citizen surveys—assessing current experiences and developing guides to good practice—and make the results widely available to local governments throughout the country.

2.   These organizations should develop training materials and training programs for public officials. The emphasis should be on proper local government applications rather than on detailed survey techniques (which are of more concern to the technician).

3.   Associations of local governments, the federal and state governments, and foundations should consider the creation and support of regional citizen survey centers. These could provide timely and inexpensive professional survey assistance to local governments in the region. The Dayton Public Opinion Center and existing university survey centers could serve as initial models for regional centers.

4.   State and federal governments should encourage citizen surveys at the local level by explicitly making surveys by local governments eligible for funding under various planning grants and revenue-sharing programs, and by identifying surveys as one aspect of citizen participation (required in connection with various federal programs).

Appendix A. An Illustrative City Services Assessment Questionnaire

This questionnaire contains illustrative questions for obtaining information on citizen experiences and perceptions of selected services provided by a local government. Such information should be used to help guide resource allocations and program and policy planning.[1]

Subjects covered by illustrative questions are:

> Section A. General Issues
> Alienation
> Overall Perception of Problem Areas

> Section B. Specific Functions
> Police
> Public Transportation
> Recreation
> Solid Waste Collection
> Health
> Environmental Quality

> Section C. Demographic Information

An individual local government considering the undertaking of a survey such as this should consider the applicability and importance of each question, make necessary revisions, determine the wording most appropriate to its own situation and pretest the questions.

---

1. These questions for the most part have *not* been tested. They are illustrative only. Neither is this appendix in actual questionnaire format—detailed interviewer instructions are not provided; responses have not been coded, etc. We have not included questions for citizen surveys on education, employment, or welfare which often are not city functions.

No attempt has been made here to seek for each function the exhaustive information that a government might obtain from citizens. Rather, the emphasis is on illustrating questions that can help in estimating the effectiveness of services and identifying major problem areas.

The complete questionnaire illustrated here is estimated to take about 30 minutes per interview.

CITIZENS SURVEY QUESTIONNAIRE

Hello, my name is _____ and I am undertaking
a survey for _____. We are interviewing
a selected sample of residents in your area to help the government better plan its
programs. We want to ask you about the city services that are provided by the city.

The information you give us will be strictly confidential and no names or
address will ever be revealed.

Section A. Questions on General Issues

Alienation

Q1. What are one or two of the main problems
in your neighborhood (considering the
neighborhood as within four blocks of your
home)?

_____

_____

Q1, Q2, Q3 and Q4 may
provide indications of
alienation of the citizens
from their government
on certain issues and
belief in accessibility to
local officials.

Q2. Thinking of these problems in the neighborhood that are important to you, do you
think the public officials in the city
(county) really do the things you want?

Most of the time ____; Some of the
time ____; None of the time ____;
No Opinion ____; Don't wish to
answer ____.

Q3. Do you feel that if you contacted someone
in the city (county) government about how
things are run, you could influence them?

On most problems ____; On some problems ____; On no problems ____; No
Opinion ____; Don't wish to answer ____.

Q4.　Did you ever contact anyone in the government about these problems?

Yes ____ ; No ____ .

Overall Perception of Problem Areas

Q5.　Here is a list of problems that some cities have. Indicate whether you feel it is a severe problem, a small problem, or not a problem at all in this city.

	Severe Problem	Small Problem	No Problem
Fear of crime			
Lack of good medical care			
Housing			
Dirty streets and sidewalks			
Garbage collection			
Unemployment			
Lack of recreation for adults			
Fires in neighborhood			
Low pay, not enough money to live on			
Lack of transportation			
Dirty air or pollution			

The statistics gathered from Q5 will inform the city officials of the major concerns of the citizens, as of that point in time. The responses will provide some relative priorities of citizen perceptions of problem areas. Note that this type of question does have some potential danger in tying the hands of government officials. However, as worded, it does not directly ask *what should be done.* However, a danger here is that this is a selective list. The latter sections of the questionnaire go into more detail on some of these areas.

	Severe Problem	Small Problem	No Problem
Drug addicts in neighborhood			
Noise in the neighborhood			
Cheating or over-charging by stores			
Lack of recreation for teen-agers			
Lack of parks			
Teenage gangs			
Care of children while parents work			
Lack of places for children to play			
Lack of good schools			
Any other (SPECIFY)			
_____			
_____			

Section B. *Questions on Specific Functions*

Police

Q6. During nighttime hours if you walked around this neighborhood, would you feel safe ____ ; safe if you are careful ____ ; or unsafe? ____

Q6, Q7 and Q8 provide data on perceptions of neighborhood and down-town safety in the streets.

Q7.   If you walked around downtown at night, would you feel safe ____ ; safe, if you are careful ____ ; or unsafe? ____

Q8.   During daylight hours when you walk around this neighborhood, do you feel safe ____ ; safe, if you are careful ____ ; or unsafe? ____

Q9.   In the last six months, have any crimes been committed against you or any member of your household?

Yes ____ , No ____ , Don't Know ____ , Don't Wish to Answer ____ .

Q9, Q10 and Q11 are a simplified illustration of questions to identify the amount of crime including un-reported crime.

RECORD RESULTS OF Q10, Q11, Q12 IN TABLE 1

(IF YES, ASK)

Q10. Please describe each crime.

Q11. Was each crime reported? (NAME EACH)

IF ANY CRIMES ARE UNREPORTED, ASK

Q12. Let me read you a list of possible reasons why the crime was not reported. Please indicate for each unreported crime, why it was not reported.

a. Afraid of what criminal might do ____
b. Didn't think it would do any good ____
c. Didn't trust police ____
d. Didn't think it was important enough ____
e. It was a private matter ____
f. Didn't want to go to all the trouble ____
g. Other (PLEASE SPECIFY) _____
_____

This is to indicate reasons for non-reporting, some of which might be reduced by government activities.

TABLE 1

Col. 1	Col. 2				Col. 3
Crime (Q10)	Reported to Police (Q11)				Reason for not Reporting — Insert Appropriate Letter (Q12)
	Yes	No	Don't Know	Won't Answer	
1					
2					
3					
4					

Q13. If you or any one in your household reported a crime, were arrested, or contacted police in any way in the last six months, please tell me how the police performed with regard to:

	Good	Fair	Poor	Don't Know	No Opinion
Politeness					
Sympathetic Handling					
Fairness					

RECORD ALL COMMENTS

Statistics based on Q13 provide information on *behavior of police* as the citizen sees it. A question that identifies these contacts as to whether the contact was originated by the household or by the police is probably also desirable to put the responses in Q13 in perspective.

Transportation[1]

Q14. How would you rate your overall satisfaction with the transportation in this city/county:

Excellent ____   Fair ____

Good ____   Poor ____

Q15. How often have you used public transit in the last month? _____

ONLY ASK Q16 IF USED PUBLIC TRANSIT

Q16. As a rider, how would you rate the transit vehicles in this city/county on the following (comfort) factors:

a) Temperature/humidity: usually comfortable ____, occasionally uncomfortable ____, often uncomfortable ____, usually uncomfortable ____?

b) Crowdedness (peak hours): almost always get a seat ____, occasionally have to stand at least part of the way ____, usually have to stand at least part of the trip ____, usually have to stand all the way ____?

c) Noisiness: quiet ____, mostly quiet ____, fairly noisy ____, very noisy ____?

d) Cleanliness: clean ____, mostly clean ____, fairly dirty ____, very dirty ____?

e) Courteous of drivers: usually very courteous ____, fairly courteous ____, unpleasant ____?

f) Odors: no problem ____, occasional bothersome fumes or odors ____, usually unpleasant ____?

Q14, Q15, Q16, & Q17 indicate: satisfaction with the overall local transportation system (Q14), ridership (Q15), perceptions of selected quality aspects of public transit (Q16) and reasons for non-use of public transit (Q17).

---

1. A more extensive list of illustrative questions is contained in Appendix D.

[IF NO TO Q15, ASK]

Q17. How would you rate the following factors as reasons why you have not used public transit for travel within this city/county in the last month?

	Major Reason	Minor Reason	Not a Reason
a) Takes too long			
b) Transit stop not close enough			
c) Transit runs too in-frequently			
d) Routes do not go to desired destination			
e) Prefer convenience of automobile			
f) Transit vehicles too uncomfortable and unpleasant			
g) Don't like crowds			
h) Too dangerous			
i) Too expensive			
j) Other (Specify)			

Recreation[2]

Q18. Recreation is sometimes thought of as the pleasant activities that are available during your free time after school or work and on weekends. What do you think of the recreation available in your neighborhood?

Very Good ____   Fair ____

Good____   Poor____

The data on the questions on recreation will provide estimates of the quality of recreation (Q18), the percentage of households using nearby recreation facilities (Q19),

2. A more extensive list of questions is contained in Appendix C.

78

and reasons for
liking or disliking
them (Q20).

DO NOT READ

No Opinion ____   Don't Know ____

IF FAIR OR POOR, ASK

Would you tell me why you say that? _____

_____

Q19. Did anyone in the household use any Public
Recreation facilities in the city during the past
month?

Yes ____   No ____   No Reply ____

What is the name and address of each?

a. _____

_____

b. _____

_____

c. _____

_____

IF YES TO Q19, ASK Q20 FOR EACH FACILITY
GIVEN

Q20. How would you or your household members rate the facilities that you have used during the past month?

Facility Name	Characteristics	Very Good	Good	Fair	Poor	Don't Know
(a)	i) Hours of Operation					
	ii) Cleanliness					
	iii) Condition of Equipment					
	iv) Helpfulness and Attitude of Personnel					
	v) Amount of Space					
	vi) Safety					
	vii) Overall Rating					

[A similar table would be provided for each facility listed in Q19.]

Solid Waste Collection[3]

Q21. What do you think of the cleanliness of your street?   Do you think the street is:

Clean ____

Mostly clean, but dirty in a few places ____

Fairly dirty ____

Very dirty ____

(Don't know or no opinion _____)

Q21 through Q23 will provide data on the quality of collection services as the consumer perceives it.

_____

3. A more extensive list of questions is contained in Appendix B.

Q22. How often do the collectors miss picking up trash and garbage on schedule? Do they:

Hardly ever miss (or never except for holidays and bad weather) ____

Miss about once a month ____

Miss more than once a month ____

(Don't know or no opinion ____)

Q23. How often do you notice widespread odors from uncollected garbage?

Hardly ever (or never) ____

About once a month ____

More than once a month ____

Q24. Have you complained to the city government about the cleanliness of streets and alleys or refuse collection services in the last six months?

Yes ____ No ____

Q24 through Q26 illustrate the use of surveys to check on the number and handling of complaints. Such questions could be used for other services as well.

Q25. How many times? _____

Q26. Were the conditions about which you complained corrected?

Always ____ Seldom if ever ____
Usually ____

Health

Q27. Did you or any member of your household use a public clinic, hospital or health referral service not paid for out of your own pocket, in the last three months?

Yes ____ No ____ Don't Know ____

These questions on health indicate the proportion of people that were treated using public funds and the difficulties

[IF YES TO Q27, ASK]

Q28. Which ones? _____

_____

[IF YES TO Q27, ASK]

Q29. Were all aspects of the service satisfactory?

        Yes ____   No ____   Don't Know ____

(IF NO TO Q29, ASK)

Q30. Let me read you a list of possible reasons why
the service was unsatisfactory. Indicate which
ones apply.

    a) It is not close enough to home ____

    b) The hours are not convenient ____

    c) Waiting times too long ____

    d) The staff are unpleasant ____

    e) Don't get helped ____

    f) Too crowded ____

    g) Other (SPECIFY) _____

_____

[IF NO TO Q27, ASK]

Q31. Let me read you a list of possible reasons why the
services were not used. Indicate which ones apply
in this case.

    a) Did not know of any service ____

    b) Service is poor ____

    c) It is not close to home ____

in being treated.
(Note that if only
the experiences of
"users" is of con-
cern, it would be
more efficient to
sample users as
drawn from
health facility
records.)

d) Prefers private____

e) Other (SPECIFY) _____

_____

Environmental Quality

Q32. In the last month, have you found your tap water. to be very good, good, fair or poor with respect to:

	Very Good	Good	Fair	Poor	Don't Know
Taste					
Smell					
Pressure					

The levels of air and noise pollution and the quality of public water are of concern to citizens.

Q33. In your daily travels in the neighborhood during the last month, have you felt that the street noise has been:

Always quiet ____

Sometimes noisy ____

Generally noisy ____

Don't know ____

Q32, Q33, and Q34 will provide citizen perceptions of the magnitude of these problems. This information supplements physical measurements.

Q34. During the last month in your neighborhood have you felt that the air has been:

Pure enough ____

Sometimes irritating to eyes or throat ____

Generally irritating to eyes or throat ____

Don't know ____

Section C. Demographic Information

Q35. In this household, tell me the ages of each member starting with the youngest.

Interviewer's
_____Tally_____

a) Less than 6 years old ____

b) 6 - 12 years old ____

c) 13 - 19 years old ____

d) 20 - 35 years old ____

e) 36 - 65 years old ____

f) Over 65 years old ____

Q36. How long have you lived in this city (county)?

_____

Q37. Do you own or rent the place you live in?

Own or buying ____

Rent ____

Other ____

CIRCLE APPROPRIATE NUMBERS

Q38. What was the highest grade in school that you completed?

0   1   2   3   4   5   6   7

8   9   10   11   12

College/Other Post High School Schooling:

13   14   15   16

Q35 through Q43 provide background data on each respondent. Answers to previous questions should be classified by these characteristics to provide indications of special problems for individual population segments. It is also desirable to check some of the statistics for the sample against census data to verify the representativeness of the sample.

Post Graduate School:

17   18   19   20   or more

Post Graduate Degree?

No 1

Yes 2

SPECIFY _____

Q39. Please tell me what your marital status is, are you single, married, separated, divorced or widowed?

Single _____
Married _____
Separated, divorced, widowed _____

Q40. And what is your age?

_____ years

Q41. What is the approximate total annual income of all members of the household including all income from wages, pension, insurance, etc., before taxes?

Under $1 thousand	_____
$ 1,000 - $ 2,999	_____
$ 3,000 - $ 4,999	_____
$ 5,000 - $ 6,999	_____
$ 7,000 - $ 8,999	_____
$ 9,000 - $11,999	_____
$12,000 - $14,999	_____
$15,000 - $24,999	_____
$25,000 - $49,999	_____
$50,000 - and over	_____

Q42. Do you consider yourself

White ____

Black ____

or, some other race? _____

Q43. What is your current address? (APPROXIMATE LOCATION WOULD BE SUFFICIENT IF RESPONDENT IS UNWILLING TO PROVIDE THE COMPLETE ADDRESS.)

_____

_____

Appendix B. Illustration of Use of Citizen Surveys for Individual Program Evaluations—An Evaluation of an Intensive Street Cleaning Campaign (See Reference1)

Name _____ Sex: M☐ F☐   Date _____

Telephone # _____   Time at start _____

Address _____   Time at end _____

Block-Face # _____   Interviewer _____

Census Tract # _____

Service Area # _____

If unsatisfactory response, why:

_____ No answer.   _____ Person no longer at this address.

_____ Telephone disconnected or   _____ Person called not in.

temporarily out of service.   _____ Could not communicate.

_____ Repeatedly busy.   _____ Person called could not answer

_____ Person no longer at this number.   at this time. Call back later.

"Hello, may I speak with Mr. (or Mrs. if woman answers telephone). I am working with the city of _____. My name is _____. I am conducting a survey to see what citizens think of the street cleaning and household refuse collection services. Would you help me by answering a few short questions? Fine."

First, do you still live at (give address) _____ ? (If yes, continue. If no, terminate.)

Now, I will ask you a question and read you several answers. Then I would like for you to tell me which answer you think is the best or most appropriate.

1. What do you think of the cleanliness of (Insert the name of the street the person lives on) Street? Do you think the street is:

_____ Clean

_____ Mostly clean, but dirty in a few places

_____ Fairly dirty

_____ Very dirty   (_____ Don't know or no opinion)

2. What do you think of the cleanliness of the alleys in your neighborhood? Do you think the alleys are:

_____ Clean

_____ Mostly clean, but dirty in a few places

_____ Fairly dirty

_____ Very dirty   (_____ Don't know or no opinion)

3. What do you think of the overall cleanliness of your neighborhood?

_____ Clean

_____ Mostly clean, but dirty in a few places

_____ Fairly dirty

_____ Very dirty   (_____ Don't know or no opinion)

4. Have you noticed any change in the cleanliness of streets and alleys in your neighborhood in the last 3 or 4 months? (If response is "No", go to #6 or #8)

_____ Yes

_____ No   (_____ Don't know or no opinion)

(If Yes)

87

5.   Are the streets and alleys now:

_____ Somewhat cleaner   _____ Somewhat dirtier

_____ Very much cleaner   _____ Very much dirtier

(Ask #6 and #7 if a special cleaning or collection operation is being evaluated. Otherwise go to #8.)

6.*   Do you know what Operation _____(Insert name of special operation)_____ is?

_____ Yes

_____ No   (_____ Not sure)

(If Yes)

7.*   Do you think Operation _____(Insert name of special operation)_____ Made a lasting effect on the cleanliness of streets and alleys:

_____ Yes

_____ No

8.   Does the city of _____ collect your trash and garbage?

_____ Yes

_____ No   (_____ Don't know. If no, or don't know, terminate unless private contractors are being evaluated.)

9.   How often do the collectors miss picking up trash and garbage on schedule? Do they:

_____ Hardly ever miss (or never except for holidays and bad weather)

_____ Miss about once a month

_____ Miss more than once a month   (_____ Don't know or no opinion.)

10.   How often do the collectors spill trash and garbage or leave some that you have set out? Do they spill or leave some:

_____ Hardly ever (or never)

_____ About once a month

_____ More than once a month   (_____ Don't know or no opinion.)

11.   How often do the collectors make so much noise that it bothers you?

_____ Hardly ever (or never)

_____ About once a month

_____ More than once a month   (_____ Don't know or no opinion.)

12.   How often do you notice widespread oders from uncollected garbage?

_____ Hardly ever (or never)   (_____ Frequently

_____ Occasionally during hot weather   (_____ Don't know or no opinion.)

13.   Have you been dissatisfied with your trash collection service at any time and for any reason in the last twelve months?

_____ Yes

_____ No

(If Yes, write in reason they gave: _____)

14.   Have you complained to the city government about the cleanliness of streets and alleys or refuse collection services in the last twelve months?

_____ Yes

_____ No

15.   How many times? _____

16.   Were the conditions about which you complained corrected?

_____ Always

_____ Usually

_____ Seldom if ever

*   For use if questionnaire is also to be used to help evaluate a special clean-up campaign.

Appendix C. Illustration of Use of Citizen Surveys by a Single Operating Agency for an Annual Assessment of Its Services—Recreation

These questions are adapted from a somewhat larger questionnaire used in June 1972 by the Recreation Department of the District of Columbia and The Urban Institute for interviewing about 700 residents of the District of Columbia. In general, the survey provided data on family participation, attitude towards quality of facilities used, reasons for not using facilities, and opinions on recreation in the neighborhood. In addition to these questions, others were included on modes of transportation, and frequency of attendance. Questions on demographic and socio-economic characteristics of respondents were also included but are not shown here.[1]

Q1. Recreation is sometimes thought of as the pleasant activities that are available during your free time after school or work and on weekends. What do you think of the recreation available in your neighborhood?

Very Good ____   Fair ____   DO NOT READ

Good ____   Poor ____   No Opinion ____

                                    Don't Know ____

IF FAIR OR POOR ASK

Would you tell me why you say that? _____

_____

[This question provides information on general perceptions of the available recreation and reasons for the attitude.]

Q2. What recreation facilities in your neighborhood did members of your household use during the past month?

[This question provides input on usage of facilities as well as providing a base for subsequent questions.]

---

1. The full questionnaire and detailed procedures and uses for the survey will be contained in a forthcoming report by The Urban Institute.

Q3. How would you or your household members rate the facilities that you have used during the past month?

Facility Name	Characteristics	Very Good	Good	Fair	Poor	Don't Know
(a)	i) Hours of Operation					
	ii) Cleanliness					
	iii) Condition of Equipment					
	iv) Helpfulness and Attitude of Personnel					
	v) Amount of Space					
	vi) Safety					
	vii) Overall Rating					

[The above question was asked about each facility that had been used by the household. It provides evaluation of various quality characteristics]

Q4. Would you give me the reasons why during the last months your household did not use the following facilities?

READ REASONS. INDICATE RESPONSE BY CHECK MARK IN BOX.

	Names of Facilities		
a. Don't know about facility or its programs			
b. Not open the right times			
c. Too far away			
d. Too crowded			
e. Not attractive			
f. Costs too much to go there			
g. Too dangerous there			
h. Do not like other users			
i. Personal health			
j. Activities not interesting IF CHECKED ASK WHAT WOULD BE INTERESTING			
k. Too busy			
l. Other (SPECIFY)			

[The Q4 questions solicited the reasons for not using facilities, which will inform management of problems that inhibit use. The facilities included here were pre-selected and were the three closest city facilities to the respondent. Some reasons can be affected by government action, others cannot. In either case, this can be important information for officials.]

Q5. Are there any recreation activities or programs that you would add or change in the city which would improve recreation for your household?

    Yes _____   No _____   Don't Know _____   No Opinion _____

IF YES

What additions or changes would you make?

_____

_____

Exhibit 5. LOCAL TRANSPORTATION SERVICES OBJECTIVES
AND ASSOCIATED MEASURES OF EFFECTIVENESS

OBJECTIVES

To provide access to community services, facilities, and employment in a safe, quick, comfortable and convenient manner for all segments of the community without causing major harmful side effects.

MEASURES OF EFFECTIVENESS

Accessibility and Convenience

1. Percent of residents not within X distance of public transit service and more than one hour from key destinations.

2. Citizen perception of travel convenience.

Travel Time

3. Time required to travel between key origin and destination points. .

4. Congestion—duration and severity of delay.

Comfort

5. Road surface quality ("bumpiness") index.

6. Citizen perception of travel comfort.

Safety

7. Rate of transportation-related deaths, injuries and incidents of property damage.

8. Number of transportation crime incidents.

Minimum Cost to Users

9. Costs per trip.

Maintenance of Environmental Quality

10. Noise level along transportation corridors and number of persons at risk.

11. Air pollution attributable to transportation sources and number of persons at risk.

General Public Satisfaction

12. Citizen perception of adequacy of transportation services.

Monetary Costs

13. Program Costs.

Source: Reference 19. These measures and data collection procedures for them are discussed in the reference.

Appendix D. Illustration of Use of Citizen Survey Information in Measuring Service Effectiveness—Local Transportation

Exhibit 5 contains a general statement of objectives for local transportation services and a list of measures of effectiveness associated with the objectives. Some of three measures (2, 6, and 12) depend on citizen surveys to obtain data for them. In addition, citizen surveys can be used to provide some information to supplement other data collection means for measures 1, 5, 8, 9 and 10. The following set of survey questions illustrate the use of survey questions to provide data on these effectiveness measures.

Illustrative Types of Questions for Citizen Survey of Local Transportation Service Quality[1]

(The particular measures of effectiveness most relevant to each type of question are shown in parentheses, e.g., M/E 12 refers to number 12 in Exhibit 5.)

A. Questions on Background of Responding Households

    1. Automobile ownership?
    2. Income class?
    3. Age of respondent?
    4. Sex of respondent?
    5. Size of family?
    6. Number in family with fulltime or part-time employment?

---

1. These are from Reference 19. Each question is relevant to a specific measure of local transportation effectiveness identified in Exhibit 5. For use in an actual survey, questions of these types would need to be carefully formulated and tested as to question wording and coverage. The wording used here is for illustrative purposes only; the questions have not been tested or prepared for questionnaire format.

7. Frequency of use of public transit/automobile for trips within the city/county: e.g., about daily, about once a week, about once a month, less than once a month?

B. Overall Quality of Transportation Service

(M/E 12) 1. How would you rate your overall satisfaction with the transportation in this city/county: excellent, good, fair or poor?

(M/E 12) 2. As compared to last year has it been getting better, worse, or about the same?

(M/E 12) 3. How would you rate your overall satisfaction with public transit within the city/county: excellent, good, fair or poor?

(M/E 12) 4. How would you rate your overall satisfaction with automobile driving conditions within the city/county: excellent, good, fair or poor?

(M/E 1 and 2) 5. Thinking of all types of trips (work, recreation, shopping, etc.), how would you rate your overall ability to get to the places you want to go within this city/county: excellent, good, fair or poor?

C. Specific Issues on Public Transit (These issues should be included in questions asked of non-users of public transit as well as users)

1. How would you rate the transit vehicles in this city/county on the following (comfort) factors:

(M/E 6) (a) Temperature/humidity: usually comfortable, occasionally uncomfortable, often uncomfortable, usually uncomfortable?

(M/E 6)	(b)	Crowdedness: almost always get a seat; occasionally have to stand at least part of the way; usually have to stand at least part of the trip?
(M/E 6)	(c)	Noisiness: quiet, mostly quiet, fairly noisy, very noisy?
(M/E 6)	(d)	Cleanliness: clean, mostly clean, fairly dirty, very dirty?
(M/E 6)	(e)	Courteousness of drivers: usually very courteous, fairly courteous, unpleasant?
(M/E 6)	(f)	Odors: no problem, occasional bothersome fumes or odors, usually unpleasant?
	2.	How would you rate the transit system in this city/county on the following (convenience) factors:
(M/E 2)	(a)	Nearness of a transit stop to home: not close enough, long walk, fairly close by?
	(b)	Routes: do not go to most places where I would want to go; too much time or too many transfers to go to most places where I would want to go; some I can get to conveniently—some I can't; routes go to most places where I want to go within the city/county?
(M/E 2)	(c)	Frequency (peak/off-peak hours): not nearly frequent enough, frequency fair, frequency satisfactory?
(M/E 2)	(d)	Information on rates and schedules: information very difficult to get, can be obtained with a little effort, readily available?
(M/E 2)	(e)	Frequency of missed schedules: frequently schedules are badly missed, occasionally missed schedules, usually on, or close to, schedule?

3. How would you rate each of the following factors as a reason that you have not used public transit for travel within this city/county (for non-users of public transit)?

			Major Reason	Minor Reason	Not a Reason
(M/E 2)	(a)	Takes too long			
(M/E 2)	(b)	Transit stop not close enough			
(M/E 2)	(c)	Transit runs too unfrequently			
(M/E 2)	(d)	Routes do not go to desired destination			
(M/E 2)	(e)	Prefer convenience of automobile			
(M/E 6)	(f)	Transit vehicles too uncomfortable and unpleasant			
(M/E 6)	(g)	Too crowded			
(M/E 8)	(h)	Too dangerous			
(M/E 9)	(i)	Too expensive			
	(j)	Other (Specify)			

4. How would you rate each of the following factors as to reasons for your non-use of automobiles for travel within the city/county?

	Major Reason	Minor Reason	Not a Reason

(M/E 1)   (a)   Don't have access to automobile

(M/E 9)   (b)   Too expensive

(M/E 6)   (c)   Too much traffic

(M/E 6)   (d)   Don't like traveling in an automobile

(M/E 1)   (e)   Can't drive; too old/ young/infirm to drive

D.   Special Issues on Automobile Travel (to be asked of both automobile users and non-users)

(M/E 2)   1.   How difficult is it usually to find parking at your destination (peak/off-peak): many places available, few places available, usually have to search for a space?

(M/E 2)   2.   How would you rate the quality of street identification signs and traffic signs and signals: satisfactory, occasionally difficult to understand, often difficult to understand, usually difficult to understand?

(M/E 5 and 6)   3.   How would you rate the quality of the road surfaces over which you ride within this city/county: generally smooth, occasionally bumpy, frequently bumpy, very bumpy?

E.   Environmental Noise

(M/E 10)   1.   To what extent have you been bothered either at home or at work by noise from motor vehicles during the past

month: not at all, on a few occasions, often, often
and with considerable annoyance?

F.   Travel Time Information

The survey can also be used to obtain information on:
estimated (limited by memory and accuracy of respondents)
walking time to transit stops (or to parking)—at both ends
of the trip, transit waiting times, and travel time (whether
by transit or automobile). If combined with information on
specific origins and destinations, total trip times can be
related to distance traveled.

Appendix E. Cover Letter for a Survey of Parents on the Local Schools

ARLINGTON COUNTY PUBLIC SCHOOLS
Office of the School Board
February, 1972

Dear Parent:

Early this school year the School Board approved the undertaking of a survey of community attitudes as another means of aiding the Board in decision-making and meeting community expectations. The survey will give you a chance to make your views known and cast a vote for the kind of schools that you want.

Enclosed is a short questionnaire that can be completed in a few minutes. The information you supply on the form will be handled in strict confidence. Signatures or other personal identification are not requested. Responses will be used only for grouped data purposes to help determine community-wide attitudes. A summary of the survey results will be published when completed. The questions appearing on the survey form were developed by a citizens committee appointed by the School Board.

Should your family receive more than one form, please complete and return only one.

Thank you for your cooperation in this effort to obtain greater knowledge of the community's attitude toward schools and education in Arlington.

Sincerely,

Chairman of the School Board

HLK:b/s
Enclosures

Appendix F. Relation Between Sample Size and Precision in a Simple Random Sample

90 Percent Confidence Intervals

If the percent giving the same answer to a question is:	And the Sample Size is:					
	50	100	200	400	500	1000
	Then there is a 90 out of 100 chance that the percent of the <u>total</u> population that would respond the same way would fall within these ranges[a]					
2	0 - 5.3	0 - 4.3	0.4 - 3.6	0.8 - 3.2	1.0 - 3.0	1.3 - 3.7
5	0 - 10.1	1.9 - 8.1	2.4 - 7.6	3.2 - 6.8	3.4 - 6.6	3.8 - 6.2
10	3.1 - 16.9	5.0 - 15.0	6.5 - 13.5	7.5 - 12.5	7.9 - 12.1	8.4 - 11.6
20	10.6 - 29.4	13.4 - 26.6	15.9 - 24.1	16.7 - 23.3	17.0 - 23.0	17.9 - 22.1
50	38.3 - 61.7	41.8 - 58.2	44.2 - 55.8	45.9 - 54.1	46.4 - 53.6	47.4 - 52.6

NOTES: 1. These apply if simple random sampling is used. If cluster sampling is used, the errors will be greater.

2. Nonsampling errors are not included.

3. These apply if the total population from which the sample is drawn is large relative to the sample size. If not, the accuracy of the sample estimate should be greater and therefore the ranges narrower than given in this table.

Source: From Reference 18. A table for 95 percent confidence intervals is also included in the reference. We suspect that the larger confidence is not necessary for the types of questions and uses by local governments.

a. More precisely, if an infinite number of samples of indicated size were taken, 90 percent of them would contain the true value of the total population in the given confidence ranges.

References and Selected Bibliography

General Information on Surveys and Their Uses

1. Blair, Louis H. and Alfred I. Schwartz, *How Clean is Our City: Measuring the Effectiveness of Solid Waste Collection Activities,* The Urban Institute, 1972.

2. Brown, Robert and Donald M. Fish, "Recreation Planning and Analysis in Local Governments," *1973 ICMA Municipal Yearbook,* 1973 (Forthcoming).

3. Carter, Launor and Ithiel de Sola Pool, "Survey Results and Public Policy Decision," *Public Opinion Quarterly,* Winter 1963.

4. "Community Issues and Action." Bank of America, San Francisco, April 1972.

5. de Berge, Earl and Conrad Joyner, "Opinion Research Comes to Tucson." *Public Management,* Vol. XLVIII, No. 10, October 1966.

6. Gallup, George and Alec Gallup, "Public Opinion Polling: America's First Research Export," *The Analyst,* May 1970.

7. Hartmann, E.L.; H.L. Isaacson and C. M. Jurgell, "Public Reaction to Public Opinion Surveying," *Public Opinion Quarterly,* Vol. 30, No. 2, Summer 1968.

8. Hatry, Harry P., Richard E. Winnie, and Donald M. Fisk, *Practical Program Evaluation for State and Local Government Officials,* The Urban Institute, 1972.

9. Kriesberg, Martin, "What Congressmen and Administrators Think of the Polls," *Public Opinion Quarterly,* Fall 1945.

10. Little, John D. C. et al, *Citizen Feedback Components and Systems,* Operations Research Center Technical Report No. 76, Cambridge, Mass.: Massachusetts Institute of Technology, 1972.

11. "Mechanized Containerized Single Family Refuse Collection," City of Scottsdale, Arizona, May 1970.

12. Nedzi, Lucien N., "Public Opinion Polls: Will Legislation Help?" *Public Opinion Quarterly,* Fall 1971.

13. Olsen, Marvin E., "Alienation and Political Opinions," *Public Opinion Quarterly,* Summer 1965.

14. "Questions Often Asked About Published Polls," *Gallup Opinion Index,* May 1970.

15. "Survey Research Needs Close CDA Monitoring," *Model Cities Service Bulletin,* July 1970.

16. Thursz, Daniel, "Community Participation: Should the Past be Prologue?" *American Behavioral Scientist,* May/June 1972.

17. "Urban Observatory Survey Report," *Nation's Cities,* August and November 1972.

18. Weiss, Carol H. and Harry Hatry, *An Introduction to Sample Surveys for Government Managers,* The Urban Institute, 1971.

19. Winnie, Richard E. and Harry P. Hatry, *Measuring the Effectiveness of Local Government Services: Local Transportation,* The Urban Institute, 1972.

20. "NEEDS," Neighborhood Environmental Evaluation and Decision System. Department of Health, Education and Welfare,

Public Health Service, Bureau of Community Environmental Management. Undated.

Survey Methods

21. Community Planning and Evaluation Institute, *A Manual on Conducting Interview Studies,* Washington, D.C., 1972.

22. de Berge, Earl and Conrad Joyner, "Opinion Polls or . . . How to Ask Right Questions of Right People at the Right Time," *Public Management,* Vol. XLVIII, No. 11, November 1966.

23. Hochstim, Joseph R., "A Critical Comparison of Three Strategies of Collecting Data from Households," *Journal of the American Statistical Association,* Vol. LXII, No. 319, September 1967.

24. MIT Operations Research Center, "Feedback on Education in the Massachusetts Public Schools," Preliminary Report to the Massachusetts Department of Education, July 1971.

25. "Residents Answer City Survey," *Public Management,* Vol. XLIX, No. 8, August 1967.

26. Saroff, Jerome R. and Alberta Z. Levitan, *Survey Manual for Comprehensive Urban Planning,* Development Research Associates, Inc., Anchorage, Alaska.

27. "Some Advantages of Telephone Surveys," *Journal of Marketing,* Vol. XX, No. 3, January 1956.

28. Selltiz, Claire, et al, *Research Methods in Social Relations,* New York: Holt, 1959.

29. Slonim, Morris J., *Sampling in a Nutshell,* New York: Simon and Schuster, 1960.

30. Stephen, Frederick F., and Philip J. McCarthy, *Sampling Opinions: An Analysis of Survey Procedures,* New York: John Wiley, 1958.

31. U.S. Bureau of the Census, *Supplemental Courses for Case Studies in Surveys and Censuses: Sampling Lectures,* Washington, D.C., 1968.

Problems of Surveys

32. Ballweg, John, "Husband-Wife Response Similarities on Evaluative and Non-Evaluative Survey Questions," *Public Opinion Quarterly,* Vol. XXX, No. 2, Summer 1969.

33. Donald, Marjorie N., "Implications of Non-Response for the Interpretation of Mail Questionnaire Data," *Public Opinion Quarterly,* Spring 1960.

34. *Federal Statistics,* Report of the President's Commission on Federal Statistics, Government Printing Office, Washington, D.C., 1971.

35. Ferber, Robert, "On the Reliability of Responses Secured in Sample Surveys," *Journal of the American Statistical Association,* September 1955.

36. Hagburg, Eugene C., "Validity of Questionnaire Data: Reported and Observed Attendance in an Adult Education Program," *The Public Opinion Quarterly,* Vol. XXX, No. 3, Fall 1968.

37. Lagay, Bruce W., "Assessing Bias: A Comparison of Two Methods," *Public Opinion Quarterly,* Vol. XXX, No. 4, Winter 1970.

38. Lenthold, David and Raymond Scheele, "Patterns of Bias in Samples Based on Telephone Directories," *Public Opinion Quarterly,* Summer 1971.

39. O'Neill, Harry W., "Response Style Influence in Public Opinion Surveys," *Public Opinion Quarterly,* Vol. XXXI, No. 1, Spring 1967.

40. Regional Plan Association, Inc., "Public Participation in Regional Planning," A Report of the Second Regional Plan, New York, N.Y., October 1967.

41. Transcentury Corporation, "Study of Recreation in the Washington Metropolitan Area," Report for the Council of Governments, January 1970.

42. Turner, Anthony, "The San Jose Methods Test of Known Crime Victims," LEAA Statistics Division, U.S. National Institute of Law Enforcement and Criminal Justice, June 1972.

43. "Winnetka/Austin: Surveys Net Citizen Response," *Public Management,* Vol. 51, No. 5, May 1969.

PUBLICATION SERIES FOR STATE AND LOCAL GOVERNMENT OFFICIALS

- *Measuring the Effectiveness of Local Government Services: Solid Waste Collection,* by Blair, Hatry, and DonVito, 1970. Proposes ways to measure health, safety, esthetics, convenience, and general public satisfaction with waste collection services. (Available only through NTIS, Springfield, Va., 22151.)
- *How Clean Is Our City? A Guide for Measuring the Effectiveness of Solid Waste Collection Activities,* by Blair and Schwartz, 1972. Elaborates how proposals in the above publication may be applied.
- *Measuring the Effectiveness of Local Government Services: Recreation,* by Hatry and Dunn, 1971. Proposes improvements in measuring accessibility, crowdedness, variety, safety, attractiveness, and degree of participation in recreation services.
- *Measuring the Effectiveness of Local Government Services: Transportation,* by Winnie and Hatry, 1972. A consumer-oriented evaluation system which emphasizes that greater attention be given to citizens who rely on public transit.
- *The Indianapolis Police Fleet Plan: An Example of Program Evaluation for Local Government,* by Fisk, 1970. Assesses benefits and costs of letting patrolman use marked police cars off-duty.
- *Options for Improving the Care of Neglected and Dependent Children, Nashville-Davidson, Tennessee: Program Analysis Applied to Local Government,* by Burt and Blair, 1971. Systematically traces the flow of children through all components of a child-care system to derive approaches for better service.
- *An Introduction to Sample Surveys for Government Managers,* by Weiss and Hatry, 1971. Offers ways to obtain reliable survey information from relatively small samples and at reasonable cost.
- *Practical Program Evaluation for State and Local Government Officials,* by Hatry, Winnie, and Fisk, 1973. Explains variety of evaluation designs and techniques and their uses.

The periodic citizen survey is a potentially valuable but seldom used means of obtaining information about the quality of local public services.

These are the kinds of questions to which local officials may obtain answers:

- How much are certain services (mass transit or recreation centers, for example) used?

- Are specific public services offered uniformly throughout the community or do they vary by neighborhood, income group, age level?

- How do users rate the services?

- Why do nonusers refrain from availing themselves of certain public services?

The authors stress the pitfalls—and how to minimize them—as well as the advantages of annual citizen surveys covering a wide range of local services.

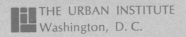

THE URBAN INSTITUTE
Washington, D. C.